UNDERAGE DRINKING:

RISKS OF DISEASE AND INJURIES

RAMESHWAR N BHARDWAJ PH.D.

Professor, George Brown College Toronto

Order this book online at www.trafford.com
or email orders@trafford.com

Most Trafford titles are also available at major online book retailers.

Print information available on the last page.

ISBN: 978-1-6987-0172-1 (sc)
ISBN: 978-1-6987-0177-6 (e)

Trafford rev. 06/09/2020

 www.trafford.com

North America & international
toll-free: 1 888 232 4444 (USA & Canada)
fax: 812 355 4082

CONTENTS

ACRONYMS/ABBREVIATIONS USED

AAF: The alcohol-attributable fraction

AFR: African Region

AUD: Alcohol use disorder

DALYs: Disability-adjusted life-years

EMR: Eastern Mediterranean Region

EUR: European Region

HED: Heavy Episodic Drinking

HUMICs: high and upper-middle income countries

LLMICs: Low and Lower Middle Income Countries

NCD: Non-Communicable Diseases

OECD: Organization for Economic Co-operation and Development

PDS: Patterns of drinking score

SEAR: South-East Asia Region

WHO: World Health Organization

WHO regions: African Region, Region of the Americas, South-East Asia Region, European Region, Eastern Mediterranean Region, and Western Pacific Region.

WPR: Western Pacific Region

ACKNOWLEDGEMENT

Every effort is made to duly acknowledge the work of scholars. We apologize for any inadvertent omission of any work used here. Please bring to our notice of any such omission/error.

EXECUTIVE SUMMARY

Alcohol plays an important role in psychiatric morbidity and is a major risk factor for other non-communicable diseases. Studies have shown that neuro-psychiatric diseases are partly and, in some cases, entirely caused by alcohol consumption. Alcohol is the substance that is most frequently abused by children and adolescents. The onset and progression of alcohol use are influenced by developmental changes in children as they enter adolescence. Medical science attests that early initiation of alcohol use leads to an increased likelihood of developing alcohol abuse or dependence in later life. In addition, compared to adults, adolescents face both higher odds of adopting persistent habits of harmful drinking and challenges from extraneous environmental factors, such as pressure from deviant peers, unhelpful family relations, parents' poor socioeconomic status, permissive societal norms regarding alcohol use, ineffective national drinking laws, and a widespread culture of nightclubs and bars. Current research estimates that approximately one-half of the risk for alcoholism comes from genetic factors and the other half from environmental risk factors. Environmental influences are deemed to have more of a role in the initiation of alcohol use, whereas genetics have more of an influence on the development of an addiction.

Harmful and hazardous use[1] of alcohol by underage youth can result in several adverse consequences for the individuals and for society. Studies indicate that alcohol use during this early period of growth may interrupt key processes of brain development, which might lead to cognitive impairment and an elevated risk of developing a chronic alcohol use disorder. Excessive and risky patterns of binge drinking by adolescents have been found to result in a greater number of unintentional injuries (e.g., traffic accidents and road injuries) for drivers in the 16 to 20 age group than for adult drivers. Furthermore, when alcohol consumption interacts with mental health conditions, such as depression and stress, it sometimes contributes to risky outcomes, such as suicide, which is estimated to be the third-leading cause of death among people between the ages of 14 and 25. Harmful alcohol

---

1   Harmful use of alcohol is defined as a pattern of alcohol use that causes damage to health. Hazardous alcohol use is defined as a pattern of alcohol use that increases the risk of harmful consequences for the user. WHO, http://www.who.int/substance_abuse/terminology/who_lexicon/en/.

use is also one of the leading causes of homicides, gang violence, sexual aggression, and street assaults. Comorbidity of alcohol use with other psychoactive substance use is also well documented.

An attempt is made in this study to estimate the quantitative contributions of harmful patterns of drinking to alcohol-attributable fractions (AAFs), using World Health Organization (WHO) data for countries in the Organization for Economic Co-operation and Development (OECD). Estimation results highlight the significant role played by the prevalence of HED (heavy-episodic drinking) among adolescents and by the level of alcoholic spirits consumed in accounting for alcohol-related deaths, injuries, and diseases. The harmful use of alcohol and drugs by adolescents imposes high health care costs, contributes to educational failure, and is likely to result in numerous other negative social consequences. With the help of evidence-based policies, most of the risk factors can be controlled, and harmful underage drinking can be checked. Preventable risk factors call for priority attention from policy makers to adopt early intervention and prevention strategies and make sustained efforts to address exposure to substance abuse during critical transitional life stages.

1

INTRODUCTION AND PROBLEM STATEMENT: ALCOHOL USE DISORDER

A lcohol is a psychoactive substance with dependence-producing properties (World Health Organization [WHO] 2014), and it plays an important role in psychiatric morbidity. It is a major risk factor for other non-communicable diseases (NCDs). Estimates from the WHO 2018 report indicate that the burden of disease (in disability-adjusted life years [DALYs])[2] associated with alcohol use disorders (AUDs) remained stagnant over the period 2000–2016, contributing 28% to total DALYs from all NCDs in each of these years. In terms of years lost due to disability (YLDs) caused by AUD, it is estimated that the disease burden increased by 9.7% (in counts) from 2006 to 2016 (GBD 2016 Disease and Injury Incidence and Prevalence Collaborators). Studies have shown that neuropsychiatric diseases are entirely or partly caused by alcohol consumption (see footnote 2). Excessive alcohol consumption[3] has been found to be responsible for an average of 79,000 deaths and 2.3 million years of potential life lost in the United States (US) each year, making it the third-leading preventable cause of death in this country (Bouchery et al. 2011).

---

2   One DALY can be thought of as one lost year of "healthy" life. The sum of these DALYs across the population, or the burden of disease, can be thought of as a measurement of the gap between current health status and an ideal health situation in which the entire population lives to an advanced age, free of disease and disability. "DALYs for a disease or health condition are calculated as the sum of the years of life lost (YLL) due to premature mortality in the population and the years lost due to disability (YLD) for people living with the health condition or its consequences" (WHO, Health statistics and information systems, https://www.who.int/healthinfo/global_burden_disease/ metrics_daly/en/).

3   Excessive alcohol consumption has been defined by Bouchery et al. (2011) as follows: binge drinking (at least four drinks per occasion for a woman, and at least five drinks per occasion for a man); heavy drinking (more than one drink per day on average for a woman, and more than two drinks per day on average for a man); any alcohol consumption by youth aged less than twenty-one years; and any alcohol consumption by pregnant women.

While alcohol use has been a part of human culture for all of recorded history, almost all societies in which alcohol is consumed are experiencing net health and social problems (Shield, Parry, and Rehm 2014). These include the growing incidence of alcohol-related diseases and injuries(Shield et al 2014); [4] the comorbid trend of alcohol use with drug use (Medina-Mora 2005); and highly risky patterns of drinking, particularly among teenagers and youth. These trends have triggered the need for control and prevention of the harmful use of alcohol. There is consistent evidence of the frequent association of alcohol consumption with the use of other psychoactive substances, particularly opioids and benzodiazepines (Peacock et al. 2018). The abuse of alcohol and other psychoactive drugs during adolescence and early adulthood poses a serious public health issue in modern societies (Hawkins et al. 1992). Binge patterns of drinking (defined as an excessive but episodic alcohol consumption pattern)[5] and underage drinking pose a grave challenge in all countries because of their adverse effects on health and their negative social consequences.

Table 1 provides a snapshot of the disease burden caused by AUDs (measured in DALYs) among adolescents and youth (age group 15 to 29) compared to adults (age group 30 to 49) at two points in time. Data show that the disease burden facing adolescents and youth increased over the period 2000–2016 while the same burden actually decreased in the older age group (30 to 49). Table 2 reports that the prevalence of heavy episodic-drinking (HED) patterns among adolescents and young people (15 to 29 years of age) and young adults (20 to 24) make up two-thirds of current drinkers in their respective age groups, demonstrating the high prevalence of binge drinking. Alcohol leads to particularly serious consequences in young people because of their higher level of vulnerability to its harmful use. There is consistent evidence that "youth who start drinking and undertake heavy drinking at a younger age are at significantly greater risk for a range of alcohol problems, including car crashes, drinking and driving, suicidal thoughts and attempts, unintentional injury, as well as drug and alcohol dependence later in life" (Friese and Grube 2010, p. 5). Over and above the direct consequences of AUD, there is a frequent association of alcohol consumption with the use of opioids and benzodiazepines (WHO 2018). Additionally, the comorbidity of alcohol and tobacco dependence tends to be strong and well documented (WHO 2018).

---

4   According to Shield, Parry, and Rehm (2014, p. 155), "Twenty-five chronic disease and condition codes in the International Classification of Disease (ICD)-10 are entirely attributable to alcohol, and alcohol plays a component-risk role in certain cancers, other tumors, neuropsychiatric conditions, and numerous cardiovascular and digestive diseases. Furthermore, alcohol has both beneficial and detrimental impacts on diabetes, ischemic stroke, and ischemic heart dis- ease, depending on the overall volume of alcohol consumed, and, in the case of ischemic diseases, consumption patterns."

5   Heavy episodic drinking (HED) is defined by WHO as sixty or more grams of pure alcohol on at least one occasion at least once per month (WHO 2018).

The OECD countries are struggling to abate the current trend of growing alcohol use and risky patterns of drinking among adolescents and youth. The population in many parts of the world is relatively young. In 2016, more than four in every ten people worldwide were younger than 25 years old (World Drug Report 2018, booklet 4). In their global study on the burden of disease and injury, Rehm et al. (2013) estimated the net effect of alcohol consumption leading to 3.8% of all global deaths and 4.6% of global DALYs attributable to alcohol in 2004. The WHO (2018) reported that while the proportion of alcohol-attributable deaths out of total deaths decreased slightly between 2010 (5.6%) and 2016 (5.3%), the proportion of alcohol-attributable DALYs remained relatively stable (5.1% of all DALYs in 2010 and 2016). The associated health cost of alcohol consumption amounted to more than 1% of the gross national product of high-income and middle-income countries in 2004, with significant additional costs of social harm not captures in these GDP figures (Rehm et al. 2013).

Alcohol-related injuries and diseases are avoidable if preventive policy interventions are in force. Preventive actions need to address harmful drinking patterns and their onset in vulnerable age groups (15 to 19). From the available evidence on AUDs and the high vulnerability of adolescents and youth to excessive drinking, three steps merit priority attention: (a) examine the multiple risk factors that influence harmful drinking patterns among young people, (b) investigate the adverse consequences of underage drinking and its associated risks of diseases and injuries, and (c) identify effective prevention strategies, using evidence-based findings.

Table 1: Disease Burden from AUDs Among Adolescents and Young People (Age Group 15–29) versus Younger Adults (Age Group 30–49) (Figures in %)

	2000	2016
People in age group - 15–29- as percentage of total population	25.9	24.18
Burden of AUDs among age 15–29 as a ratio of total NCD DALY in age 15–29	3.01	3.02
People in age group- 30–49- as percentage of total population	26.2	27.0
Burden of AUDs among age 30–49 as a ratio of NCD DALY in age 30–49	3.16	2.56

Note: NCD refers to Non-communicable Diseases
Source: WHO Database on Disease Burden

Table 2: World Trends in Prevalence (in %) of HED by Adolescents (Age Group 15–19 and Young Adults Age Group 20–24) Among Drinkers

	Prevalence Among Drinkers (%) 2000	Prevalence Among Drinkers (%) 2016
Age Group Pop. 15–29	49.3	45.7
Age Group Pop. 20–24	52.3	48.5

Source: Table 3.6 in WHO (2018): Global Status Report on Alcohol and Health

PLAN OF THE STUDY

To address the issues outlined above, this study is organized into five sections. The first section compiles evidence about the prevalence of alcohol use, particularly among young adults. This section also briefly discusses the consequences of episodic drinking. As there is a wide geographical variation in the proportion of alcohol-attributable deaths and DALYs, section 2 presents data about alcohol use and alcohol related disorders by WHO regions and age groups. Regional variation in drinking pattern is tested by two-way ANOVA procedure. Section 3 estimates the factors that lead to alcohol-attributable fractions (AAFs). Section 4 deals with preventive policies to reduce the harmful use of alcohol and the alcohol-attributable health and social burden in a society. The study is concluded in Section 5.

2

PREVALENCE OF ALCOHOL USE AND ALCOHOL-RELATED DISORDERS BY REGION AND AGE GROUP

Alcohol is used far more often than any other drug. The 2016 GBD study (GBD 2016 Alcohol Collaborators 2018) produced detailed evidence on alcohol and drug use and disorders in 195 countries. The following broad observations were reported. First, among all the psychoactive substance use disorders (SUDs), AUDs have been found to be the most prevalent as of 2016, with an age-standardized prevalence of 1,320.8 cases per 100,000 people, followed by the next most common drug use disorder, cannabis dependence, with an age-standardized prevalence of 289.7 cases per 100,000 people. Second, it has been noted that among the population aged 15 to 49 years, alcohol use was the leading risk factor globally in 2016, with 3.8% of female deaths and 12.2% of male deaths attributable to alcohol use in this age group (GBD 2016 Alcohol Collaborators 2018). Third, on a global basis, alcohol use ranked as the seventh-leading risk factor for premature death and disability in 2016, compared with other risk factors in the GBD studies. For men, alcohol use has been identified as the fourth-ranked risk factor causing early death and disability in 2017 (Institute for Health Metrics and Evaluation 2018). Another daunting finding is that alcohol abuse and dependence suffers from the widest treatment gap,[6] at 78.1%, among mental disorders and SUDs (Kohn et al. 2004).

---

6   The "treatment gap" (TG) refers to the difference that exists between the number of people who need care and those who receive care(Kohn et al 2004)

2.1 PREVALENCE OF ALCOHOL AND DRUG USE AMONG ADOLESCENTS AND YOUTH

Alcohol and drug use data are regularly available from the Global Information System on Alcohol and Health, WHO, ESPAD surveys for Europe, and the Monitoring the Future (MTF) series for the US. The sixth survey in the ESPAD series and the forty-first survey in the annual MTF series report similar trends for substance use among teenagers and youth. In the US, the survey by MTF[7] in 2018 revealed a downward trend in the use of illicit drugs and heavy consumption of alcohol by school students in grades eight, ten, and twelve since the peak period of 1997, but the survey offered a note of caution that there has been a growing perverse perception among teenage populations in that they are seeing occasional drug use as less likely to represent a problem or a risk (MTF 2018). More troubling results for the US show that the age at onset of alcohol use has been decreasing over the last 35 years, with youth now initiating drinking at 12 years on average and the median age at onset of SUDs being around 15 years of age (Castellanos-Ryan et al. 2013). The findings (from the MFS follow-up surveys in 2000) demonstrate the common co-occurrence of tobacco use, illicit drug use, and risky sexual behavior among heavier users (Windle 2003). However, the 2015 ESPAD Report, which collects and monitors data about alcohol and drug use among 15- to 16-year-old students in European countries, reports that over the last two decades (1995–2015), there has been an overall decrease in the prevalence of alcohol use in a lifetime from 89% to 81%; they also reported a decrease in alcohol use "over the prior 30 days" from 56% to 47%, (2015 ESPAD Report).

Alcohol is consumed by more than half of the population in only three WHO regions: the Americas, Europe, and the Western Pacific (WHO 2018). The highest levels of per capita alcohol consumption are observed in countries of the WHO European region (WHO 2018; GBD 2016 Disease and Injury Incidence and Prevalence Collaborators; Lancet 2017). Not only is underage drinking illegal, this pattern of drinking among adolescents and youth is also associated with a significant public health impact in terms of negative consequences, such as injury, accidents, alcohol-related dependence, and disease burden.

Average rates of drinking mask large differences across individual countries regarding risky levels of drinking (HED). Moreover, it is the age at onset of drunkenness that raises special concerns. In the ESPAD survey, about one-fifth of students in Estonia, Latvia, the Russian Federation, and Slovakia reported having experienced their first intoxication by age 13 years or younger. The impact of alcohol consumption on chronic and acute health outcomes in populations is largely determined by two separate but related dimensions of drinking: total volume of alcohol consumed and pattern of drinking (WHO 2018). The

---

7   MTF is a long-term study of substance use and related factors among US adolescents, college students, and adult high school graduates through age fifty-five.

available data show significant differences among countries in regard to drunkenness or binge patterns of drinking. The discussion below presents a brief review of the recent trends in order to enable a more detailed understanding of the nature of underage drinking and its prevalence in different WHO regions.

HEAVY EPISODIC (BINGE) DRINKING PATTERNS AMONG ADOLESCENTS AND YOUTH

Although adolescents drink less often than adults do, they are particularly vulnerable to binge drinking (HED) because, as per medical science, their impulse control has not yet fully matured (Juergens and Hampton 2019). Adolescence is considered a unique developmental period of malleable brain and body maturation (Crew et al. 2016).

HED or binge drinkers are defined as males who consume five or more alcoholic drinks in a row and females who consume four or more in a row, over a two-hour period (Siqueira and Smith 2015). Results of school surveys (ESPAD; GSHS8) indicate that in many countries, alcohol use starts early in life—especially before the age of 15 years (WHO 2018). Global evidence suggests that as with the prevalence of current drinking, the prevalence of HED increases between age 15–19 years and 20–24 years. However, in all regions of the world, HED peaks in the 20–24 age group and is higher than in the total population (WHO 2018).

Table 3, which presents global and regional data, shows that the prevalence of HED increases between ages 15–19 years and 20–24 years. Table 4, which displays the regional profile of risky drinking, substantiates that the highest HED rates among young people of both sexes in the 15–19 age group have been found in the European region (24.1%, males: 36.2%; females: 11.5%), the region of the Americas (18.5%, males: 30.1%; females: 6.4%), and the Western Pacific region (18.8%, males: 30.0%; females: 6.4%). Similar trends are also visible for youth across regions in the 20–24 age group (Table 5 below).

The above epidemiological evidence is corroborated by several country-level studies in the Americas and Europe. Analyzing the alcohol-drinking cultures (such as social drinking norms) of European adolescents, Bräker and Soellner (2016) found that an average of 15% (SD = 7.53) of adolescents (in the 12–16 age group) across all countries could be classified as "risky users." These authors found that 11 countries belonging to the third cluster (which includes the Central European countries)[8] had the highest proportion of (heavy) episodic users compared with the other clusters. The WHO data on excessive drinking by underage populations reveal that Luxembourg topped the list of places where 15- to 19-year-olds engaged in HED in 2016.

---

8   Central and European countries include, The Netherlands, Germany, Switzerland, Austria, Belgium, Poland, Italy, Slovenia, Denmark, Finland and Ireland

Table 3: Regional and Global Estimates of Prevalence of HED 2016: Age Group 15–19

WHO Regions and World	Heavy Episodic Drinking Among Adolescents (Percentage of Drinkers) Age 15–19
AFR	55.1
AMR	49.3
EMR	10.9
EUR	51.2
SEAR	46.8
WPR	49
World	45.1

Source: WHO Global Status Report on Alcohol and Health 2018

Table 4: Regional and Global Estimates of Prevalence of HED 2016: Age Group 20–24

WHO Regions and World	Heavy Episodic Drinking Among Adolescents (Percentage of Drinkers) Age 20–24
AFR	57.4
AMR	51.8
EMR	10.9
EUR	54.7
SEAR	49.9
WPR	51.8
World	45.8

Source: WHO Global Status Report on Alcohol and Health 2018

Evidence confirms that younger people are more likely to engage in HED than mature adults (OECD 2015). SAMHSA (2014) reported that among the Americans in the 12–20 age group, 14.2% reported binge drinking in 2013. In their study of underage and adult drinking behavior in the US, Foster et al. (2003) reported that underage drinking and excessive adult drinking accounted for 50.1% of alcohol consumption and 48.9% of consumer expenditure on drinking in 1999. The socio-environmental reasons suggested for the increased drinking trend among young people include the low cost of alcoholic beverages, the wider availability of alcohol, forms of alcohol promotion designed to target younger drinkers, and changes in the acceptability of drinking in many OECD countries (OECD 2015).

While there are divergent HED trends across countries, the overall evidence indicates that after a steep increase in underage drinking, countries have started experiencing a declining trend in the prevalence of heavy-drinking sessions around the new millennium. Table 5, which has been reproduced from the WHO (2018), indicates that since 2000, the HED prevalence among young people has been decreasing worldwide or, in the case of the WHO South-East Asia and Western Pacific regions, has at least remained stable. IARD (2019)[9] research indicates that Europe experienced a decline in HED by more than 25% between 2005 and 2016. In regard to the US, Pedersen and von Soest (2015) conducted an 18-year trend study that showed that after a steep increase in the 1990s, binge drinking decreased by the same magnitude after the turn of the century. Lipari et al. (2017) also found that between 2008 and 2014, underage binge drinking by people aged 12 to 20 declined in the US from 19.3% in 2002 to 13.8% in 2014.

Table 5: Trends in Prevalence of HED Among Adolescents and Youth

WHO Regions	Age 15–19 Years (%)		Age 20–24 Years (%)	
	2000	2016	2000	2016
AFR	17.3	12.7	26.9	20.8
AMR	25.8	18.5	36.3	28
EMR	0.4	0.2	0.9	0.5
EUR	35.1	24.1	46	33.9
SEAR	10.2	10.2	17.4	17.6
WPR	18.1	18.8	27.2	28.2
World	17.1	13.6	25.8	21.8

Source: WHO Global Status Report on Alcohol and Health 2018

The reduction in both rates of consumption and the associated negative health outcomes has been the result of aggressive programs and evidenced-based prevention initiatives adopted in countries in the last two decades. It should be cautioned, however, that the relationship between AUDs and other psychoactive substances cannot be ignored. In other words, alcohol use data should not be viewed in isolation from other psychoactive substances. As indicated earlier, alcohol and drug use have been found to be quite a common occurrence among adolescents and youth (Swendsen et al. 2012; Storr et al. 2013). Johnston et al. (2018) reported in regard to US adolescents and youth that many engage in illicit drug use occasionally and a few do so regularly. Heavy episodic use is not as common but reflects the most dangerous behavior, combining the risk resulting from frequent intake with that

---

9   International Alliance for Responsible Drinking (IARD), a not-for-profit organization, is dedicated to reducing harmful drinking and promoting understanding of responsible drinking.

of consuming large amounts of alcohol (Bräker and Soellner 2016). The co-occurrence of alcohol use and drug use disorders poses a higher risk of a greater severity of substance dependence. The following subsection compares the disease burden associated with AUDs, as well as with combined psychoactive substances across various geographical regions.

2.1.1 DISEASE BURDEN FROM ALCOHOL USE DISORDERS (AUDs)

Globally, AUDs are ranked as the most prevalent of all SUDs, with an age-standardized prevalence of 1320.8 cases per 100,000 people (GBD 2016 Alcohol and Drug Use Collaborators; Peacock et al. 2018). Alcohol use from preadolescence through young adulthood is a major public health challenge for countries. Youthful drinking is associated with an increased likelihood of alcohol abuse or dependence in later life. The risky use of alcohol, or "alcohol misuse," is used as a collective term to encompass alcohol dependence and harmful alcohol use (National Collaborating Centre for Mental Health, United Kingdom [UK] 2011). AUDs comprise alcohol dependence and the harmful use of alcohol (Atlas on Substance Use 2010; WHO). Table 6 presents data on alcohol dependence and the harmful use of alcohol across different regions. As seen from the table, alcohol dependence (the most severe form of AUD) occurred in 2.6% of people aged 15+ years in 2016 at the global level; it was most prevalent in the region of the Americas (4.1%) and the European region (3.7%).

Table 6: Alcohol Dependence and Harmful Use of Alcohol: Past 12 Months' Prevalence of AUDs (Percentage of the 15-year-old+ Population, 2016)

WHO Regions	Alcohol Dependence	Harmful Use
AFR	1.3	2.4
AMR	4.1	4.1
EMR	0.4	0.4
EUR	3.7	5.1
SEAR	2.9	1.0
WPR	2.3	2.3
World	2.6	2.5

Source: Global status report on alcohol and health 2018, WHO

HED and underage drinking are associated with a high burden of disease consequences, such as high rates of morbidity, mortality (WHO 2018), alcohol dependence, and co-occurring physical and mental health problems early in life. Scientific investigations of the adolescence developmental period support the hypothesis that adolescent binge drinking leads to long-lasting changes in the adult brain that increase the risk of adult psychopathology, particularly for alcohol dependence (Crews et al. 2016). Robust empirical evidence suggests higher odds of risk regarding substance abuse and dependence faced by adolescents who engage in binge drinking than those who do not binge drink (Monico 2019; Filmore and Jude 2011; McCarty et al. 2004; Viner and Taylor 2007; Conrad et al. 2008).

As a leading risk factor for death and disability among people aged 15–24 years, Lancet (2018) estimates from the WHO (2018) affirm that alcohol accounted for a large burden of disease and injury in 2016, representing 5.1% of all DALYs10 in that year. Regarding mortality risk from alcohol consumption, the same WHO (2018) report estimated that these deaths were greater than those from tuberculosis (2.3%), HIV/AIDS (1.8%), diabetes (2.8%), hypertension (1.6%), digestive diseases (4.5%), road injuries (2.5%), and violence (0.8%). Of all the deaths in the 20–39 age group, alcohol-attributable deaths accounted for approximately 13.5% (WHO 2018). The disease burden estimates by Rehm et al. (2009) indicated that 4.6% of global DALYs were attributable to alcohol.

Alcohol use in adolescence has been reported to be associated with huge economic and social costs, which may include academic failures, health care expenditure, diminished work capacity at an early age, loss of worker productivity, criminal justice system expenses, property damage from motor vehicle crashes and fires, and special education needed for those with fetal alcohol spectrum disorders (Siqueira and Smith 2015). At the individual level, substance abuse causes mental illness and the impairment of cognitive processes (dependence and deficits in cognitive functions). In the long run, the dependence causes social dysfunction, unemployment, disability, and death. Both alcohol use and associated mental illness are major global risk factors for disability and premature loss of life, bringing significant social and economic losses to individuals and society at large (WHO 2018). Another worrisome trend is that 44.8% of total recorded alcohol consumed worldwide comes in the form of spirits,[10] followed by beer (34.3%) and wine (11.7%).

REGIONAL LANDSCAPE OF ALCOHOL-USE DISORDERS (AUD)

The distribution of the AUD burden is quite uneven among the countries in each region. Tables 6 and 7 clearly suggest substantial regional variations. Per the 2016 GBD study, the prevalence of AUDs has been the highest for countries/regions with a high social

---

10   Spirits contain the highest percentage (40%) of pure alcohol equivalent(WHO 2011, Global status report on alcohol and health).

development index (SDI).[11] The table above shows AUDs being the highest in the European region (8.8% of the population of age group 15+). In their findings on the epidemiology of alcohol-attributable deaths in Europe, Rehm et al. (2011) found that about 25% of the difference in life expectancy between Western and Eastern Europe for men aged 20–64 years in 2002 could be attributed to alcohol largely, but not exclusively, as a result of differences in HED patterns. Within the European region, Central, Eastern, and Western Europe consistently recorded not only higher alcohol consumption per capita (11.64, 11.55, and 11.13 liters, respectively) but also a higher percentage of heavy consumption among drinkers (49.5%, 46.9%, and 40.2%, respectively) (Peacock et al. 2018). In their comparative study of substance abuse, Degenhardt et al. (2016) corroborated that alcohol has caused the heaviest health burden in Eastern Europe. Comparing the alcohol-drinking culture among adolescents in European countries, Bräker and Soellner (2016) found that Central European countries showed the most problematic behavior when "episodic," "frequent," and "heavy episodic users" were classified as "risky users," while Western European countries showed the least.

The next highest AUD burden is found in the region of the Americas (representing 8.2% of the population aged 15 years and older). The highest prevalence rates of AUDs in the population in parts of Eastern and Central Europe (reaching up to 16% in some countries) is followed by the Americas (reaching up to 10% for some countries in this region), Southeast Asia, and some countries in the Western Pacific (rates reaching up to 13%) (see Atlas on Substance Abuse 2010; WHO, Ch. 1). Spirits are the leading drink in Eastern Europe, Central and North America, and most of Asia. Spirits contain 40% pure alcohol equivalent, compared to 11%–16% in wine and 4%–5% in beer (OECD Health Statistics 2018).

At the global level, alcohol-attributed unintentional injuries, digestive diseases, and AUDs have been observed to be the leading contributors to the disease burden and were individually responsible for 30.0%, 17.6%, and 13.9%, respectively, of all alcohol-attributable DALYs (WHO 2018, p. 65). Risky patterns of alcohol use by adolescents contribute to significant adverse economic costs and social loss. Comparing the economic costs attributable to alcohol in selected high- and middle-income countries, Rehm et al. (2009) demonstrated that the economic costs of alcohol were substantial in both groups,

---

11   The Socio-demographic Index (SDI) is a summary measure of a geography's socio-demographic development. It is based on average income per person, educational attainment, and total fertility rate (TFR). SDI contains an interpretable scale: zero represents the lowest income per capita, lowest educational attainment, and highest TFR observed across all GBD geographies from 1980 to 2015, and one represents the highest income per capita, highest educational attainment, and lowest TFR. The SDI is the geometric mean of total fertility rate, income per capita, and mean years of education among individuals aged fifteen years and older; it was included as a composite measure of develop- mental status in GBD 2016. Global Burden of Disease Collaborative Network. Global Burden of Disease Study 2015 (GBD 2015) Socio-Demographic Index (SDI) 1980–2015. Seattle, United States: Institute for Health Metrics and Evaluation (IHME), 2016.

ranging from $3581 in Scotland to $ 8371in the US. Middle-income countries, such as Korea ($524 I), compared to the alcohol-attributable cost per capita in low-income countries. Adolescent binge drinking is also associated with significant adversity and social exclusion in later life (Viner and Taylor 2007). Of the total estimated economic cost of excessive drinking in 2006, binge drinking accounted for 76.4% (Bouchery et al. 2011), and more than 40% of binge drinking-related costs were paid by the government (Sacks et al. 2015).

Table 7: Age-Standardized Alcohol-Attributable Disability-Adjusted Life Years (DALYs) per 100,000 People (2016)

Age-Standardized Alcohol-Attributable DALYs per 100,000 People						
AFR	AMR	EMR	EUR	SEAR	WPR	World
3043.7	1821.9	322	2726.5	1718.3	1132.9	1758.8

Source: WHO Global Status Report on Alcohol and Health 2018

2.1.2 THE COMBINED EFFECT OF ALCOHOL AND DRUG USE: DISEASE BURDEN FACING ADOLESCENTS AND YOUTH

Alcohol and other drugs have long been consumed for recreational purposes (GBD 2016 Alcohol and Drug Use Collaborators). Alcohol and drug use cause a substantial disease burden globally, and the composition and extent of this burden varies strongly with sociodemographic development (GBD 2016 Alcohol and Drug Use Collaborators). Rohde et al. (2001) reported that adolescent AUD significantly predicted AUDs, SUDs,[12] depression, and elevated levels of antisocial and borderline personality disorder symptoms by age 24. Comorbid disorders can be seen among youth during the transition to young adulthood (aged 18 to 25) (NIDA 2018). Swendsen et al. (2012) found that alcohol and drug use were common in US adolescents, and the findings of their study indicated that most cases of abuse have their initial onset in this important period of development.

Considering alcohol use data along with drug use, the calculations in Table 8 indicate that the total burden attributable to substance use increased from 8.12% in 2000 to 8.46% in 2016 at the global level for people in the 15–29 age group (i.e., adolescents and young people). Among the WHO regions, the same trend of increased disease burden from

---

12 Substances can be divided into three major categories: Alcohol, Illicit Drugs (a category that includes prescription drugs used non-medically), and Over-the-Counter Drugs. In this document, over the counter drugs are not con- sidered.(U.S. Department of Health and Human Services (HHS), Office of the Surgeon General, Facing Addiction in America: The Surgeon General's Report on Alcohol, Drugs, and Health. Washington, DC: HHS, November 2016).

substance use is observed in all regions, with the exception of Europe, which experienced a decline from 14.9% in 2000 to 13.7% in 2016. However, as shown in Table 8, both Europe and the Americas are facing high disease burdens due to SUDs. The finding of a higher disease burden due to substance use in Europe and the Americas compared to the world average is reinforced by the fact that "the burden due to drugs increased with higher SDI level" (GBD 2016 Alcohol and Drug Use Collaborators, p. 987).

Comparing the burden from AUDs to drug use among countries, the GBD 2016 Alcohol and Drug Use Collaborators further added that alcohol-attributable burden was highest in countries with a low SDI and middle–high SDI, whereas the burden due to drugs increased with a higher SDI level. Regarding drug use disorders, the above GBD report noted that the regions where drug use accounted for the highest proportion of DALYs were high-income North America (5.2 million DALYs, or 5.1% of all DALYs), Eastern Europe (3.0 million DALYs, or 3.4% of all DALYs), and Australasia (203,000 DALYs or 3.1% of all DALYs) (GBD 2016 Alcohol and Drug Use Collaborators p. 998).

Alcohol and drug misuse are comorbid disorders that require serious attention. Young people suffer disproportionately from premature mortality due to alcohol, with the proportion of all deaths attributable to alcohol consumption being greatest among those who are 20–39 years of age (WHO 2018). Most research around the globe testifies that early (12–14 years) to late (15–17 years) adolescence is a critical risk period for the initiation of substance use and that substance use may peak among young people aged 18 to 25 years (UNODC 2018, booklet 4). Adolescence is considered the key period of development of SUDs, with striking increases in SUDs across adolescence into early adulthood (Merikangas and McClair 2012). The study by Whiteford et al. (2013) on the global burden of disease found that while the burden of mental disorders and SUDs spanned all age groups, the highest proportion of DALYs occurred in adolescents and young- to middle-aged adults (aged 10–29 years).

Table 8: Trends in DALYs Attributable to Alcohol and Drug Use Disorders: Age Group 15–29 (2000 and 2016) (Percentage of Total DALYS Attributable to Non-communicable Diseases in the Same Age Group)

WHO Regions	DALYs Attributable to Alcohol Use Disorders 2000	DALYs Attributable to Alcohol Use Disorders 2016	DALYs Attributable to Drugs Use Disorders 2000	DALYs Attributable to Drugs Use Disorders 2016
AFR	2.28%	2.73%	2.61%	3.18%
AMR	4.75%	3.24%	8.25%	10.16%
SEAR	2.2%	2.19%	2.87%	3.46%
EUR	5.89%	5.6%	9.04%	8.12%
EMR	1.46%	1.72%	4.83%	5.91%
WPR	2.66%	2.91%	5.78%	5.56%
World	3.01%	3.02%	5.11%	5.43%

Source: Calculations Based on Estimates of Disease Burden, 2000–2016, WHO, Health Statistics and Information Systems

VULNERABILITY FACTORS

Various individual- and environmental-level factors make adolescents vulnerable to AUDs. These factors include stress-engendered negative emotions (Cooper et al. 2005), age and development history (Babor et al. 2017), family history of alcoholism, high impulsivity (Poikolainen 2000), conduct problems, personality characteristics, genetic markers (Cheng et al. 2004), neuropsychological problems (Cheng et al. 2004), peer and other social relations (Chartieret al. 2010), unregulated alcohol marketing and promotion activities exposing adolescents and youth to potentially harmful contents (Babor et al. 2017), school dropouts, and disengaged youth (Manhica et al). Figure 1 below provides a simplified and synoptic view of the vulnerability factors, such as age, individual-level characteristics, and wider socio-environmental factors. Individual-level characteristics, such as personality and genetics, interact with experiences and exposure to socio-environmental factors and directly affect the developing brain's structure and function (UNODC 2018). Studies confirm that social norms and the surrounding environment, among other factors, exert a powerful influence on what people believe to be acceptable drinking behaviors (UNOCD 2018).

Evidence from OECD countries shows that NEET ('not in employment, education or training') youth have a higher propensity for substance abuse than other young people (Godfrey et al. 2002). Evidence related to school dropouts in the US shows that

12th-grade-aged youth who had dropped out of school were more likely than similarly aged youth who were still in school to engage in current cigarette use, alcohol use, binge alcohol use, marijuana use, nonmedical use of psychotherapeutic drugs, and use of any illicit drugs (Tice 2013). Data also show that current substance use rates among 12th-grade-aged male dropouts were higher than the rates among similar-aged males who were still in school (Tice 2013). A study of Mexican youth revealed that NEET youth were the prime targets of exploitation by organized drug-peddling gangs (Benjet et al. 2012). Windle (2003) found that when comparing alcohol use and its burden among a nationally representative sample of 12th-grade students in regular schools with those in alternative schools,[13] rates of alcohol use were considerably higher for the latter than the former and were in the same range as other health-compromising behaviors, such as drinking and driving, suicide attempts, and engaging in unprotected sex leading to unintended pregnancies and sexually transmitted diseases (Windle 2003). Failure to complete high school education lowers socioeconomic status, which, in turn, raises the intergenerational risk of children's socioeconomic and educational attainment (Tice et al. 2017).

Figure 1: Vulnerability Factors Facing Young Adults

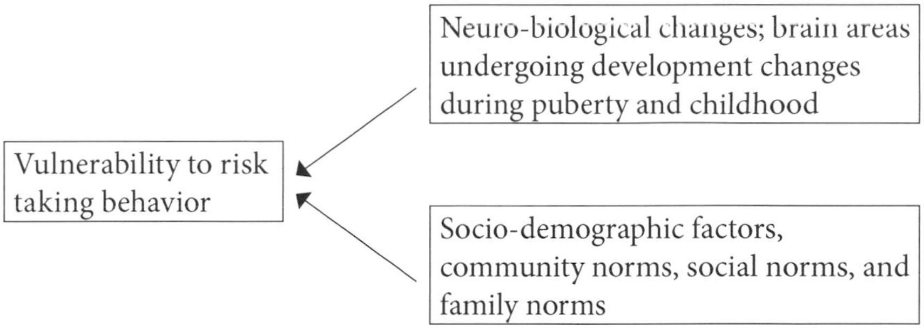

Sources: Adapted from Balogh, K.N., Maryes, L.C., and Potenza, M.N. (2013). Gu, J., Hawkins, J. D., Hill, K. G., and Abbott, R.D.(2001).

Drinking patterns can differ for each community and can be associated with diverging standards of monitoring and surveillance efforts by public regulatory bodies. Additionally, the role of public and community efforts in minimizing school dropouts and eliciting parents' involvement in the matter of changing perceptions of underage drinking is well documented by researchers. As shown above, regional evidence (based upon WHO data) quite clearly indicates that alcohol use during adolescence and its escalation in frequency and density of consumption in later years is quite a common trend among North American and European countries.

---

13   The term alternative schooling refers to nontraditional public and private educational approaches available by choice to parents and students.

An attempt is made in this study to explore the relationship between alcohol use by adolescents and the prevailing regional characteristics (economic development levels and underlying region-specific environment), using WHO data. The following discussion presents empirical estimates using the two-way ANOVA (Analysis of Variance) procedure.

2.2 ANALYZING REGIONAL VARIATIONS: EXPLORATORY STATISTICAL ANALYSIS USING ANOVA

The initiation of alcohol use at an early stage and its hazardous use (binge-drinking pattern) are a worrying trend for developed nations that are concerned about the future of the youth. Statistical explorations of regional variations in the harmful[14] use of alcohol can be used to find some evidence of the roles of the region-specific broad environment and relative economic affluence. An attempt is made to quantify and compare certain aspects of drinking patterns across Europe and North America, and the relative influence of economic affluence. This exercise will help us to obtain information about underage drinking problem in regions(Europe and North America) where underage drinking is a normative behavior(Beccaria and White 2012). For the two-way ANOVA[15] that is used here, it is postulated that region-specific environmental factors (such as socio-cultural norms and the national policy factors implicit within them) and the relative level of economic affluence among regions are independent factors that abet or moderate the harmful use of alcohol. The present study focuses on countries in the two regions that have the highest per capita alcohol consumption and the riskiest pattern of alcohol use: Europe and the Americas. These independent variables (factors) are categorical/dummy variables (Field 2016).[16]

Two-way ANOVA can be conceptualized as a regression equations of the following form:

Heavy Episodic Drinking = $\beta_0 + \beta_1$ Region (Europe or Americas) + β_2 Economic development level Category + β_3 Interaction term (Region* development-level category) + e

---

14   Harmful use of alcohol is defined as periodic heavy drinking and drinking to intoxication (Ahlström et al. 2004).

15   ANOVA is an extension of the independent-samples t-test and can be used to compare any number of groups or treatments. The purpose of an ANOVA is to test whether the means for two or more groups are taken from the same sampling distribution. When we have determined whether the means of three or more groups are different, analysis of variance (ANOVA) is a suitable choice compared to t-test. ANOVA analysis is conducted by comparing the variance (or variation) between the data samples to variation within each particular sample. If the between variation is much larger than the within variation, the means of different samples will not be equal. If the between and within variations are approximately the same size, then there will be no significant difference between sample means. ANOVA uses F-tests to statistically test the equality of means.

16   See Field (2016) to see how the data needs to be recorded. Also see the SPSS commands in Field.

Underage Drinking = b0 +b1 Region (Europe or Americas) + b2 Economic development Category + b3 Interaction term (Region* development-level category) + ε

STATISTICAL OUTPUT FROM TWO-WAY ANOVA

To check the ANOVA's assumptions of equal variances (Homogeneity of Variances) and normality, Levene's Test is used. In Table 9, nonsignificant result (see sign = 0.144) indicates that we fail to reject the null hypothesis that the variances are all equal. This implies that the homogeneity-of-variance assumption is being met. We notice from Table 9 that the F-ratio is highly significant, which means that region-specific factors (ignoring regional economic development) significantly influenced underage drinking.

Table 9: Levene's Test of Equality of Error Variances

Dependent Variable: Prevalence of Underage (15–19 Years) Drinking

F	Df1	Df2	Sign
2.191	1	63	0.144

This result is supported by several international studies that have examined the influence of social norms and related factors, such as alcohol availability and pricing, on alcohol consumption among adolescents and young adults (Ahlström et al. 2004). More liberal drinking-age laws, permissive social attitudes (including perceptions of more liberal parental attitudes), and retail distribution systems appear to foster early initiation of alcoholic beverage consumption in Europe (Friese and Grube 2001; Moore et al. 2010). Ahlström et al. (2004) noted that in European countries, more than half of 11-year-olds reported having tasted alcohol, compared to the average age of about 13 years for first-time alcohol users in the US. Friese and Grube (2001) found that "not only do youth in the majority of European countries report a higher prevalence of intoxication, they also are more likely to report intoxication before age 13."

Additionally, the results in the table10 indicate that if we ignore the region-specific influences, then underage drinking behavior is also impacted by the level of economic affluence. This result is supported by international evidence from 195 countries and territories that found that alcohol use has been generally higher among higher-SDI quintiles (GBD 2016 Alcohol Collaborators 2018). Drinking prevalence was lowest in low-to middle-SDI locations.

Table 10 does not indicate a significant effect of the interaction between region-specific influences and the level of economic affluence on underage drinking behavior.

In reality, there are several factors that complicate comparisons among countries and regions. There are large differences across individual countries in terms of frequency, quantity, and intoxication levels. Some countries show a drinking culture which is geared more toward intoxication, while the drinking culture of other countries is characterized by drinking more frequently but also more moderately (Beccaria and White (2012). The evidence from several research studies (Beccaria and White 2012) support our finding that in Europe and North America, there is relatively high rates of drinking, drunkenness, and HED among adolescents. High-income countries generally have the highest alcohol consumption rates (WHO 2014).

Table 10: Tests of Between-Subject Effects

Dependent Variable: Prevalence of Underage (15–19 Years) Drinking

Source	Type iii sum of squares	df	Mean square	F	Sgn
Corrected model	15272.875a	3	5090.958	64.187	0.000
Intercept	92184.370	1	92184.370	1162.264	0.000
Regional classification (Americas and Europe)	3464.812	1	3464.812	43.684	0.000
Development-level classification	3752.114	1	3752.114	47.307	0.000
Regional effect*Development-level effect	15.676	1	15.676	0.198	0.685
Error	4838.183	61	79.314		
Total	157301.680	65			
Corrected total	2011.058	64			

Note: $R^2 = 0.759$ (Adjusted $R^2 = 0.748$)

Under-age drinking raises several public health and social concerns. The causal links between alcohol and death, disease and injury is well established (WHO 2011, 2014, 2018). Most adverse health effects from underage drinking stem from acute intoxication resulting from binge drinking. Underage binge drinking is associated with several health risk behaviors and contributes to the three leading causes of death- unintentional injury, homicide, and suicide- among persons aged 12 to 20 years (Miller et al. 2007). It has been found that adolescents who binge drank were more likely than both nondrinkers and current drinkers who did not binge to report poor school performance and involvement in several health risk behaviors. Estimates show that 4% of all deaths worldwide are attributable to alcohol. The harmful use of alcohol is especially fatal for younger age groups

(WHO 2011). Alcohol is the first substance used during adolescence, and its use is often associated with progressive experimentation with other illicit drugs (Stewart et al. 2005).

In the next section, an attempt is made to quantify the health and social risks associated with harmful pattern of drinking, with a focus on countries of Europe and Americas where alcohol consumption among adolescents has become a "major public health and social concern" (OECD 2015).

3

ALCOHOL-RELATED HEALTH EFFECTS AND INJURIES: CROSS-SECTIONAL EVIDENCE

T here is a causal relationship between the harmful use of alcohol and a range of mental and behavioral disorders, other NCDs, and injuries (WHO 2018). The WHO report (2018) has hypothesized a causal model of alcohol consumption and health outcomes, as depicted in Figure 2 below. In the following model, alcohol consumption can result in three types of health and social outcomes.

At the individual level, alcohol consumption has been found to be leading risk factor globally causing mortality/deaths: 3·8% (95% UI 3·2–4·3) of female deaths and 12·2% (95% UI 10·8–13·6) of male deaths attributable to alcohol use among the population aged 15–49 years (GBD 2016 Alcohol Collaborator report). The volume of alcohol consumed (including the percentage of spirit content of alcoholic beverage) and the pattern of alcohol use (including episodic and binge style of drinking). Episodic drinking to intoxication greatly increases the risks of accidents, injuries, violence, and heart diseases (Connor et al. 2016). Additionally, alcohol and substance use are associated with mental illness, impairment of cognitive processes, and dependence. In the long run, dependence causes social dysfunction, unemployment, disability, and death. Beyond health consequences, the harmful use of alcohol results in significant social and economic losses for the society at large (WHO 2018). Social consequences and harm to others may be in the form of serious road injuries, educational failure and dropout, juvenile crime, and treatment and rehabilitation costs to the public. Epidemiological studies indicate that adolescents and younger age groups face a relatively greater risk for alcohol abuse than people in other age groups. In regard to the vulnerability of age to the risk of alcohol use, Crews et al. (2016) remark, "Adolescents are more sensitive to alcohol disruption of cognition than adults, further increasing risks of accidents, heavy binge drinking, and unwanted consequences. Blackouts are common among adolescents, consistent with heavy binge drinking." It is estimated that for each 0.02% increase in blood alcohol concentration (BAC), there is a greater increase in fatal-crash risk for younger drivers than for those aged 21 years. This 'age' sensitivity effect coupled with thrill seeking and peer/social factors can promote extreme binge drinking and very high blood alcohol levels (Courtney and Polich 2009).

Among young people, the male population has been found to be facing higher odds of alcohol use than the female population in the same age group. The WHO (2018) study reported alcohol use as the leading contributors to the burden of alcohol-attributable deaths and DALYs among men were injuries, digestive diseases, and AUDs, whereas among women, the leading contributors were cardiovascular diseases, digestive diseases, and injuries (WHO 2018). Among the societal-level factors, level of economic development and culture of drinking have also exerted significant influence on the pattern and volume of alcohol consumption by the population. In general, the greater the economic wealth of a country, the more alcohol is consumed and the higher prevalence of HED among drinkers (WHO 2018). Moreover, it has been observed that globally, the difference in sex ratio of current drinking decreases with economic status (WHO 2014). Rehm et al. (2009) demonstrated that in high- and middle-income countries, the economic costs attributable to alcohol and those attributable to AUDs were substantial and comparable. Cultural and situational factors that influence the behavior of young people toward drinking include: alcohol used to celebrate achievements social events, and family activities; easy availability of alcohol in retail grocery stores; and its low price. There is overwhelming evidence for the primacy of sociocultural factors in determining harmful drinking pattern. At a societal level, the European Union is the heaviest-drinking region in the world, with over one-fifth of the European population aged 15 years and above reporting heavy episodic drinking (5 or more drinks on an occasion, or 60 grams of alcohol) at least once a week. This heavy episodic drinking is widespread across all ages and all of Europe, and not only among young people (WHO 2018).

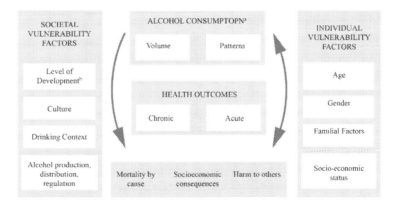

[a] Quality of the alcohol consumed can also be a factor
[b] Development of health and welfare system and economy as a whole
Source: Based on Rehm et al., 2010 and Blas et al. 2010

Figure 2: Conceptual Causal Model of Alcohol Consumption and Health Outcomes
Source: Reproduced from WHO (2018), Alcohol: Key Facts

3.1 GLOBAL ESTIMATES OF ALCOHOL-ATTRIBUTABLE HARMS

Alcohol is a unique risk factor by virtue of the sheer number of diseases, injuries, and social harms with which it is associated (WHO, Regional office of Europe 2019). This report further adds that the overwhelming majority of alcohol-attributable mortality is found in four broad categories: cancer; cardiovascular disease (CVD), liver disease (with mainly liver cirrhosis as a cause of death), and injury. The burden of disease and injury attributable to alcohol use represented 5.1% of all DALYs in 2016 (WHO 2018). Globally, AUDs are the leading cause of injury (Gentilello et al. 2005), resulting in both unintentional road injuries and intentional injuries. Taken together, these injuries account for more than a third of the burden of disease attributable to alcohol consumption, which includes injuries from traffic crashes, burns, poisoning, falls, drowning, and violence against oneself or others (WHO 2009). Globally, in 2016, 4.2% of all DALYs were attributable to alcohol use (GBD 2016 Alcohol and Drug Use Collaborators, Lancet Psychiatry 2018). Moreover, this Lancet study also shows that the global DALYs attributable to alcohol use were highest for injuries. Using emergency department data from different countries, Cherpitel et al. (2015) reported that 16.4% of all injuries are attributable to acute alcohol use between 2001-2011 in their 18-country sample.[17].

As per the WHO report (2009), "Alcohol affects individual psychomotor skills involving brain–eye–hand–foot coordination. The effect on visual focus, reaction time and judgment leads to injuries from causes like motor vehicle accidents and falls. Alcohol intoxication also has an effect on an individual's cognitive skill" (p. 3). Furthermore, adolescents are more sensitive to alcohol-related disruption of cognition than adults, which further increases the risk of accidents, injuries, and unwanted consequences (Crews et al. 2016). Alcohol-related injuries affect not only those who are intoxicated at the time of injury but also those who fall victim to their behavior. Internationally, it is estimated that 10%–18% of injured patients admitted to the emergency department had consumed alcohol prior to the injury (Korcha et al. 2013).[18] For the US, it is estimated that around

---

17   Calculation of alcohol-attributable fraction (AAF) of injury is based on the following formula (Cherpitel et al. 2015):

$AAFi = Pi$ (Alcohol | injury $x(1-($Alcohol | injury x (1- 1/RR), where Pi represents the proportion of the population exposed in group i and RRi is the relative risk of mortality in exposed group i compared with the reference group (in alcohol often non-drinkers or lifetime abstainers). See WHO (2009) for objective and subjective estimates of AAF (p. 34).

18   To study the risk of injury associated with drinking, studies use the data on injured people in hospital emergency departments (EDs). EDs have been considered to be an ideal place to sample injury patients seeking treatment, and many studies have used medical-condition (non-injury) patients as control subjects. Emergency department controls are assumed to be from the same geographic area as cases and to possibly share some other similar characteristics such as socioeconomic status (WHO 2009, p. 18). Emergency department studies, in

two-thirds of trauma cases result from unintentional causes, while violence accounts for one-third of traumatic injuries.[19] Per this committee (see footnote 18) on trauma, statistics prove that up to 50% of reviewed patients in emergency departments are dependent on alcohol, compared to 7%–8% of the general population. Injury related to violence caused by alcohol consumption is a serious concern. Cherpitel and Ye (2010) found that the risk of a violence-related injury due to drinking prior to the violent incident is over five times greater than the risk from drinking for injuries due to other causes. A strong association has been found between alcohol use and injuries resulting from violence, and much of the literature documenting this association has come from studies conducted in hospital emergency rooms, where patients admitted for violence-related injuries are significantly more likely to have a positive BAC and to report drinking prior to the violent event than patients sustaining injuries from other causes (Cherpitel and Ye 2010).

The findings by the WHO (2009, Ch. 1) suggest that the risk of alcohol-related injury is not only due to HED but also to chronic high-volume drinking and is highest when both conditions are met. Taylor, Shield, and Rehm (2011) found from their empirical exercise that AAFs for injury mortality decrease with age and increase as binge drinking increases. Cherpitel et al. (2015) have also reported a similar result of estimated AAFs being higher in those countries with the most harmful (detrimental) drinking patterns, which exhibit a high prevalence of heavy drinking. Most alcohol is consumed on heavy-drinking occasions, which increases all risks of alcohol-related diseases and injuries (WHO, Regional Office for Europe 2012). This report further adds that "in particular, heavy drinking occasions are a cause of all types of intentional and unintentional injuries, and of ischemic heart disease and sudden death" (P 1). In regard to drinking and traffic injuries, it was found that the risk of a traffic crash starts at low levels of BAC and increases significantly when the driver's BAC is ≥0.04 g/dl.[20] At any BAC, drivers aged 16 to 20 years are three times more likely to crash than drivers who are older than 30 years.[21]

Based on the above empirical findings and the causal model of alcohol consumption (Figure 2) in health and social consequences, the present study has made an attempt to provide an empirical estimate of the relationship between the detrimental pattern of drinking across countries/regions and the alcohol-attributable fractions (AAF).

---

which data are collected from injured patients on factors related to their injury and alcohol use, provide a unique opportunity to examine the causal role of alcohol in injuries. Acute alcohol involvement among those injured can be compared to a control group to determine the relative risks for injury associated with alcohol (WHO 2009, chap. 3 for details on methodological aspects).

19   American College of Surgeons Committee on Trauma (undated) Alcohol and Injury Presented by the Subcommittee on Injury Prevention and Control.

20   https://www.who.int/news-room/fact-sheets/detail/road-traffic-injuries.

21   World report on traffic injury prevention 2004, Geneva, World Health Organization.

3.1.1 EMPIRICAL ESTIMATION OF RISK FACTORS FOR ALCOHOL-ATTRIBUTABLE FRACTIONS (AAF)

This section investigates the quantitative relationship between AAF and alcohol consumption using cross-sectional data from 88 countries in Europe and the Americas. Given the fact that alcohol is consumed by more than half of the population in only three regions of the world–the Americas, Europe and Western pacific (WHO 2018)–the study focusses on Europe and Americas.[22]

International comparisons of alcohol consumption and its consequences can be used to 1) relate per capita consumption to certain alcohol–related outcomes and 2) to evaluate changes of both consumption and different outcomes within a country or across countries over time (Bloomfield 2003). Research evidence indicates that the average volume of alcohol consumed, drinking patterns (e.g., heavy-drinking occasions), and the quality of alcoholic beverages consumed are likely to have a causal impact on mortality and morbidity related to chronic diseases and conditions (Shield, Parry, and Rehm 2014). Alcohol consumption is estimated to be a causal factor in more than 200 disease and injury conditions (WHO 2018, Alcohol, Key Facts).

In the literature, the AAF indicator is used to quantify, at the population level, the contribution of alcohol to all diseases and injuries for which it is known to be causally related (Martin et al. 2010).

AAF is the proportion of the cases recorded in a population with a particular condition that is deemed to be caused by alcohol (Martin et al. 2010). Its calculation enables the estimation of the proportion of cases of a disease or type of injury that may be attributed to the consumption of alcohol. In alcohol epidemiology, the AAF is defined as the proportion of disease that would disappear if alcohol consumption decreased to zero (Taylor, Shield, and Rehm 2011). AAF is calculated as a positive function of the prevalence of drinking (the exposure) and the relative risk function of each alcohol-related condition (the disease risk) (Jones et al. 2008).

In the statistical exercise below, AAF is modelled as a log linear function of PDS (pattern of drinking score) and regional factors (Europe versus Americas).

Model: $L_n(AAF) = \alpha + \beta_1(PDS) + \beta_2 D$

where, AAF is a measure of the proportion of deaths from various causes that are directly or indirectly attributable to alcohol consumption; Ln=natural log of AAF; PDS=risky pattern of drinking score, which takes the value 1(less risky) to 5 (more risky); D=1, if Europe, D=0, if not Europe)

---

[22] This is because these regions comprise of countries where teenage drinking is more prevalent compared to countries in the other WHO regions. Comparisons of countries in these regions present cross-cultural pattern of drinking that are especially valuable when evaluate the effectiveness of different policies.

The aim of the exercise is to determine the role of the risky pattern of drinking in causing alcohol-attributable adverse health outcomes. The log-linear model, specified above, has a logarithmic term on the left-hand side of the equation and untransformed (linear) variables on the right-hand side. A log linear model is used here since the dependent variable, AAF, has extreme values for certain East European countries. If we examine the data on the alcohol–attributable fractions (AAFs) (as a percentage of all deaths), we observe that alcohol-related deaths in some European countries (such as Republic of Moldova, Belarus, Lithuania, Russia, and Lativa) had been nearly 3 to 4 times the average AAFs in other countries in our sample (WHO 2018, P 367-370). In a log linear model, logarithmic transformation has the effect of making larger values less extreme (Griffiths et al. 2012, Ch 4, section 4.5). Logarithmically transforming variables in a regression model is commonly recommended to handle situations where a non-linear relationship exists between the independent and dependent variables (Benoit 2011). Using the antilogarithm transformation results in an exponential function (Griffiths et al. 2012, Ch 4).

Variables Selection

The selection of explanatory variables is based on the evidence from popular research studies (Rehm et al. 2010; Connor et al. 2016; Bouchery et al. 2011; Connor et al. 2015; WHO 2018). Pattern of drinking (e.g., excessive alcohol drinking on certain occasions) has been found to be an important determinant of premature death, increased disease and injury, alcohol-related crime, etc. in several studies (WHO 2009, 2014, 2018; Bouchery et al. 2006). European nations, with their highest levels of alcohol consumption in the world, continue to have the highest share of all deaths and morbidity attributable to alcohol consumption (WHO 2010, Regional Office of Europe; WHO 2019, Regional Office of Europe).[23] These two explanatory variables (pattern of drinking score and region-specific grouping–European nations versus non-European nations) are briefly enumerated below.

(i) Pattern of Risky Drinking. One explanatory variable is the risky drinking pattern, represented by PDS (pattern of drinking score), which is a composite measure developed by the WHO (2018) that reflects how people drink on a scale of 1 (least risky pattern of drinking) to 5 (most risky pattern of drinking).

(ii) The influence of Regional Factors. Throughout the world, numerous different drinking cultures and attitudes toward alcohol exist (Bloomfield et al. 2003). The estimation utilizes cross-sectional data on 88 countries belonging to the regions of Europe and Americas. These regions vary in terms of several region-specific factors, such as

---

23 WHO, Regional Office of Europe (2010): "Fact sheet on alcohol consumption, alcohol-attributable harm and alcohol policy responses in European Union Member States, Norway and Switzerland".

alcohol-related policies (legal minimum drinking age; pricing and accessibility of alcohol; and retail outlets) and quality of alcohol consumed (including homemade spurious drinks). Evidence shows that the European region (including the EU) has not only the highest prevalence rate of alcohol drinking among 15–19-year-olds, many countries in this region have also scored relatively low on reducing the negative consequences of drinking (in terms of the reported AAF (WHO 2018). To capture the influence of region-specific factors, region-specific dummies are introduced to account for the additional variability in AAF.

Estimation Results

Before discussing the results, a brief discussion on the adequacy of the sample size of 88 countries is first presented. There are two common rules of thumb: 10 cases of data for each predictor in the model, or 15 cases of data per predictor. In our estimation, sample size is quite adequate, even by another criterion of 50+8k, where k is the number of predictors (See Field 2009, Ch 7).

The following tables report the output from the log-linear regression model used to analyze the alcohol-attributable AAF. Tables 11a and 11b present information about the fitness of the model. In these tables, the model summary and ANOVA output data reveal that the log linear specification fits well with the data.

Table 11: Log-Linear Model

Table 11a: Model Summary

Model	R	R Square	Adjusted R Square	Std. Error of the Estimate	Sig. F Change	DW
1	.827a	.685	.677	0.272	00.00	1.59

a. Predictors (Constant), Dummy Eur=1, Others=0. PDS Score

Table 11b: ANOVA

Model	Sum of Squares	df	Mean Square	F	Sig.
Regression	12.884	2	6.442	86.822	<.001b
Residual	5.936	80	.074		
Total	18.820	82			

Dependent Variable: Natural Log of AAFs, Predictors.
Constant, Dummy Eur=1, Others=0 PDS Score

Table 11C: Co-efficient

Model	Unstandardized Coefficients		Standardized Coefficients	t	Sig.	Collinearity Statistics	
	B	Std. Error	Beta			Tolerance	VIF
1 (Constant)	0.520	0.102		5.096	<.001		
PDS (Pattern of Drinking)	.349	.028	.780	12.425	<.001	.999	1.001
Eur=1, Others=0	.285	.060	.297	4.726	<.001	.0.999	1.001

a. Dependent Variable: Natural log of AAF

A commonly used measure of the goodness of fit provided by the estimated regression equation is the coefficient of determination. The ratio r^2 = SSR/SST is called the coefficient of determination.[24] In our estimation, r^2 =0.685 (Table 11a), indicating that 68.5% of the of the total variance in the dependent variable is explained by the independent variables. In ANOVA, Table(11b), an F-test based on the ratio MSR/MSE[25] is used to test the statistical significance of the overall relationship between the dependent variable and the set of independent variables. The results of the overall F-test (p<0.001, Table 11b) indicate that the independent variables reliably predict the dependent variable.

To test the normality of the residuals, we can look at the histograms and normal probability plot (Field 2009, Ch 7). The normality assumption is justified when the histogram looks like a bell-shaped curve (normal distribution). To assess whether or not the data set is approximately normally distributed, normal probability plot (graphical technique) is used to examine the deviation of observed residuals around a straight line (which represents a normal distribution). In this plot, typically, the y-axis is the residuals (or standardized) and the x-axis is quintiles of the standard normal. In our case, the normality assumption is not violated by the data.[26]. To check the linearity[27]

---

24   SST=total sum of squares=SSE+SSR. SSR=regression sum of squares; SEE=residual sum of squares. Residuals are the differences between the values of the outcome predicted by the model and the values of the outcome observed in the sample. SST = total variation in the observed response (dependent variable), which can be written as the sum of two parts: $y_i - \bar{y} = (y_i - \hat{y}_i) + (\hat{y}_i - \bar{y})$.

$$\text{SST} = \Sigma(y_i - \bar{y})^2 + \text{SSE} = \Sigma(y_i - \hat{y}_i)^2 + \text{SSR} = \Sigma(\hat{y}_i - \bar{y})^2$$

25   MSR=mean square due to regression= SSR divided by degrees of freedom; and MSE-mean square error= SSE by its degrees of freedom

26   The graph is not shown in the text here.

27   Statistical tests used in the regression model are based on the following assumptions regarding the error term, ε (1) ε is a random variable with an expected value of 0; (2) the variance of ε is the same for all values of

and homoscedasticity, we can examine the residual plot (residuals on the y-axis and the predicted values on the x-axis). Another alternative to check linearity is to use scatter plots (plot of the dependent variable/or residuals on the y-axis and the independent variable on the x-axis). If the points are randomly and evenly dispersed throughout the plot, this pattern is indicative of a situation in which linearity and homoscedasticity are met (Field 2009). In our case, this assumption is met.[28]

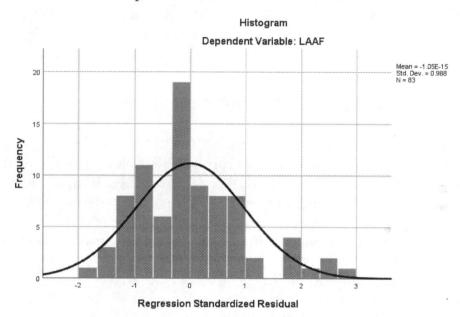

Histogram
Dependent Variable: LAAF

Mean = -1.05E-15
Std. Dev. = 0.988
N = 83

Table 11c indicates the absence of any serious multicollinearity problem. Multicollinearity is a problem when the R^2 between any predictor and the remaining predictors is very high. One indicator of collinearity is the variance inflation factor (VIF) statistic. Because the VIF is simply the reciprocal of the tolerance, very low values of tolerance (0.1 or less) and very high values of VIF (10 or more) indicate a problem. Since the VIF statistic is around 1 in our exercise, it confirms that collinearity is not a problem here.

Interpretation of the Coefficients

In the table of coefficients (11c), the results of the t-statistics show that each of the explanatory variables in the model, PDS(t(80)=12.425, p<0.001) and region-specific dummies(t(80)=4.726, p<0.001), make a significant contribution to the model. The

---

x; (3) the values of ε are independent; and (4) ε is a normally distributed random variable (See Encyclopedia of Britannia, Section: Experimental designs).

28   Graph not shown in the text here.

explanatory variable PDF has a coefficient, $\widehat{\beta_1} = 0.349$, which can be interpreted as $(\partial \ln(AAF))/\partial PDS$, holding regional effect unchanged. This indicates that for every unit increase in PDS, Ln(AAF) would increase by 0.349 units, after controlling the regional effect. Thus, by fixing the regional effect, we find that $\Delta \log(\widehat{AAF})^\circ = \widehat{\beta_1} \Delta PDF$.[29]

The coefficient on the European region (represented by dummy=1) measures the average difference in AAF between Europe and Americas, facing the same level of PDF (See Wooldridge 2013, Ch 7, example 7.1). That is, if we take the same level of PDS for both regions, the European region, on an average, exhibits 33% (that is, 100*[exp(0.285)-1]) higher AAF than that resulting from alcohol consumption in the Americas.

3.2 DISCUSSION OF FINDINGS

In our study, the dependent variable is the log of AAF (Alcohol-attributable fractions). AAF is considered one of the best methods currently available at quantifying the harms and benefits due to alcohol consumption (World Health Organization, 2000). [30]A high volume of alcohol consumption and its use in detrimental patterns (such as episodic forms of drinking) pose a serious endemic risk for alcohol-related deaths and morbidity and injuries. The quantitative evidence in our study endorses this pathetic problem. It is found that large values of PDS (high score of risky pattern of drinking) exert a positive and significant influence on AAF in the countries included in our study. Several research studies have found a robust link between alcohol consumption with non-communicable diseases. Covering a time period of 16 years (from 2000-2016) and 195 locations, the Lancet study (GBD 2016 Collaborators, 2018) found that the risk of all-cause mortality, and of cancers specifically, rises with increasing levels of consumption, and the level of consumption that minimizes health loss is zero. The consumption of 50 or more grams of alcohol per day has been found to lead to at least a two-to-three times greater risk of developing these cancers than nondrinkers (NIH website, Alcohol and Cancer Risk). Every 10 grams of alcohol consumed per day has been associated with a 12 percent increase in the risk of breast cancer (NIH website). The same NIH site has also reported that, compared to occasional or non-drinkers, the risk of colorectal cancer increases by 1.5 times

---

29   To get the exact percentage change in the predicted AAF owing to a unit increase in PDF, we need to use the formula $\%\Delta((\widehat{AAF}))^\circ = 100*[\exp(\widehat{\beta_1})-1]$, where $\exp(\widehat{\beta_1}) \approx 1+\widehat{\beta_1}$ (see Wooldridge 2013, Benoit 2011). This implies that a unit increase in PDS (that is, moving to a risky pattern of drinking) is likely to result in 100*[exp(0.349)-1]=42% increase in AAF. This result follows from the algebraic properties of the exponential and logarithmic functions (See Wooldridge 2013, Ch 6). $\exp(\beta_i) \approx 1+\beta_i$ is an approximation for small values of β_i (Benoit 2011). For a more detailed derivation and explanation, see Griffiths et al. 2012, section 4.5.

30   World Health Organization (2000): "International guide for monitoring alcohol consumption and related harm." Department of Mental Health and Substance Dependence."

among people who regularly drink 50 or more grams of alcohol per day. The WHO (2014) report found that half of cirrhosis mortality worldwide can be attributable to alcohol, and a higher rate of approximating 60% in North America and Europe. Manthey et al. 2017 has reported a strong high correlation (>0.9) between the crude mortality rate of alcoholic CM (cardiomyopathy) and the AAFs. Moreover, heavy episodic drinking among underage people (15-19 age group) has been found to be associated several social harms such as road injuries, homicides, violence and school drop-outs (WHO 2018).

In addition to examining the association between risky pattern of drinking and negative health and societal harms, the study also tests the role and significance of regional environment factors (that may include drink culture, enforcement of legal restrictions, minimum age laws, retail distribution network, unregulated markets) on AAF. Since the per capita alcohol consumption in the WHO European Region, including the European Union (EU), is the highest in the world, this results in proportionally higher levels of burden of disease attributable to alcohol use compared to other regions (WHO 2019, Regional office for Europe). This finding is corroborated in several research studies. One ignominious aspect of alcohol consumption at the global level is that a quarter of this consumption (24.8%) has been found to be unrecorded, that is, homemade alcohol, illegally produced or sold outside of normal government controls. Comparing unrecorded alcohol consumption practices among European countries, Papova et al. (2007) have indicated that the unrecorded use of harmful hepatoxic alcohol in CEE and eastern neighbors (viz.,Crotia, Hungary, Maldova Republic, Romania, Slovenia, and Ukraine) can be linked to increasing mortality from alcoholic liver diseases-cirrhosis.[31]

Another factor is the lower legal minimum age for buying alcohol. In many European countries, the minimum legal drinking age is 18. In contrast, the national minimum legal drinking age in the US is 21, which is a primary alcohol-control policy in that country. The age of onset of drinking alcoholic beverages has been found to be associated with engagement in multiple risk behaviors (including, smoking, substance abuse, frequency of alcohol drinking, criminal offending, violent behavior, road injuries, and mood disorders) during early and late adolescence (WHO 2004, MacArthur et al. 2012). Lower drinking age also results in higher episodes of binge drinking compared to countries with higher legal minimum drinking age (Wechsler & Nelson 2010). The WHO (2009, Ch. 18) report also reinforces the above result for the European Union (EU), where alcohol-related injuries

---

31   Four broad categories of unrecorded alcohol can be distinguished: 1) homemade alcoholic beverages (legal and illegal); 2) illegally produced alcohol and/or counterfeit alcoholic products, or informally produced alcohol that was not declared to state authorities to avoid taxation; 3) alcoholic products not or not officially intended for human consumption but consumed as surrogate alcohol (such as medicinal or cosmetic alcohols); and 4) alcohol that is brought across the border (smuggled or legally brought, but registered in another jurisdiction), WHO 2019, Regional office for Europe.

are found to carry a high proportion of disability and premature death across Europe, especially among 15- to 29-year-olds.

Another contributor to higher alcohol attributable AAF in Europe relates to the type of alcoholic beverage commonly used. In Europe (more particularly, Eastern Europe), there is an excessive consumption of distilled spirits. High per capita distilled spirits consumption has been found to be the strongest determinant of the adult male mortality rate in Europe as soon as we acknowledge the unrecorded alcohol consumption (Korotayev et al. 2018). The findings of Coder et al. (2009) suggest that, among hospitalized problem drinkers, drinkers of spirits were most likely to have diseases, followed by those that drank beer (WHO 2014). Additionally, countries in Eastern Europe also have practices of having a relatively higher level of unrecorded alcohol consumption that includes illegally-distributed alcohol as well as homemade or surrogate alcohol, not intended for consumption by humans (e.g., cosmetics containing alcohol). Lachenmeier et al. 2014 have argued that such illegally-produced spirits regularly contain higher percentages of alcohol (above 45% by volume).

3.3 NEED FOR PUBLIC ACTION

Evidence of alcohol-attributable diseases, premature mortality, injuries (roads and violence), and other societal harms calls for evidence-based public policies to tackle the risk factors for early onset of drinking. Early intervention strategies encompassing early detection and population-based prevention programs hold great promise in reducing risks for initiation of alcohol use at the adolescence stage. In many cases, alcohol use is an individual choice, driven by social norms, with strong cultural connotations (OECD 2015). Geographical variations in alcohol attributable deaths is wide (OECD 2015). High risk levels and pattern of consumption are largely concentrated in high- and higher-middle-income countries. In the US, the American Academy of Child and Adolescent Psychiatry has reported that among those 15 to 24 years of age, 50% of deaths (from accidents, homicides, and suicides) involve alcohol or drug abuse. The highest AAF is in the WHO European region (WHO 2018). Environmental factors play quite an influential role in determining attitudes and drinking behavior. Some such environmental conditions include community drinking norms, the degree of enforcement of legal minimum drinking-age laws, messages from media (advertising), the influence of corporations in political decision-making, alcohol accessibility factors governed by national regulations concerning licensing of sale, distributional networks, national policies about restrictions for on-site consumption (e.g., bars and cafés), and off-premise sales (e.g., stores and supermarkets) of alcoholic beverages.

The following appendix to this section uses 'Ordinal Regression' model for predicting risky factors of drinking.

APPENDIX TO SECTION 3

PREDICTING RISKY PATTERNS OF ALCOHOL DRINKING: ORDINAL LOGIT MODEL

To prevent alcohol-related harm, it is important to understand what constitutes risky patterns of drinking. There are, however, many conceptual and methodological challenges to defining risky drinking (Dawson 2011). In his view "the most essential challenge lies in determining the threshold that discriminates "low-risk" and "risk" drinking."(P144). The risk of alcohol drinking is informed by knowing how frequently alcohol is consumed and the number of drinks per occasion (i.e., their drinking patterns) (WHO 2014). Based largely on the concept of "binge" patterns of drinking (also known as heavy episodic drinking that brings blood alcohol concentration (BAC) to a higher than the safe level), WHO (2014, 2018) has developed a measure on an ordinal scale called PDS–the pattern-of-drinking score. PDS defines a scale of risky behavior, with one representing the least risky pattern of drinking and five representing the riskiest pattern of drinking (WHO 2014). PDS estimates are based on the following six drinking attributes, which are weighted differentially in order to scale the PDS from one to five (WHO 2014, p. 35):[32]

- the usual quantity of alcohol consumed per occasion;
- taking part in festive drinking;
- proportion of drinking events in which drinkers get drunk;
- proportion of drinkers who drink daily or nearly daily;
- drinking with meals; and
- drinking in public places.

Another significant source of alcohol-related risk is the drinking of unregulated homemade alcohol, for which reliable estimates are not available. The types and quality of liquor consumed and the practice of mixing different types alcoholic beverages by youth can also raise the risk to health. There is lack of consensus about determining precisely the cut off limit between safe and risky levels and patterns of drinking. This uncertainty surrounding the safe level is echoed in a large-scale global study in 2018. GBD 2016

---

32   This discussion draws upon WHO (2014). According to this report, two of these attributes make the pattern of drinking less risky—namely, the proportions of drinkers who drink with meals or those who drink daily or nearly daily.

Alcohol Collaborators (2018), analyzing levels of alcohol use and its health effects in195 countries between 1990 and 2016 concluded that there was, in fact, no safe level of alcohol consumption. They found that the risk of all-cause mortality, and of cancers specifically, rises with increasing levels of consumption.

There is also considerable variability in alcohol content within and across beverage type (e.g., beer, wine, and distilled spirits), and considerable differences in the rates of spirit use among youth in countries in this sample. Evidence also indicates that the severity of the alcohol-related consequences not only depends on the volume of alcohol consumption over time, but also on the pattern of drinking, and in some regions, such as Russia, on the quality of the alcoholic beverage (Papova et al. 2007). The pattern of drinking spirits in consuming countries (such as the 'vodka culture' in Eastern European countries) can be characterized by non-daily drinking, irregular binge drinking episodes (e.g., during weekends and at festivities), and the acceptance of drunkenness in public (Papova 2007). Mäkelä et al. (2011) argue that the form in which the alcohol is consumed has an influence, particularly in societies where there are patterns of extreme intoxication. For example, spirits are sometimes called "shots," which can be a single spirit, or two or more mixed together, and are designed to be drunk in one go, and so it hits the blood stream very fast. Liquor, compared to wine and beer, are often masked in larger drinks, such as soda or juice, which can make it easier for individuals to consume drastically more alcohol in a very short period of time. Evidence, thus, support that youth who reported usually consuming liquor were also more likely to report frequent alcohol consumption and binge drinking than students who reported consuming other types of alcoholic beverages (Naimi et al. 2015, Gonzaleset et al. 2011). On the basis of the above reasoning, the consumption of spirits has been considered as a factor influencing the PDS. Another possible predictor of PDS score is the country's level of economic affluence. Evidence shows that, in general, the greater the economic wealth of a country, the more alcohol is consumed and the smaller the number of abstainers. High-income countries have been found to have the highest alcohol per capita consumption (APC) and the highest prevalence of heavy episodic drinking among drinkers (Cook, Bond & Greenfield 2014, WHO 2014, WHO 2018). With rising incomes and increasing consumer purchasing power, along with more intensive marketing of branded alcohol beverages in high and upper middle-income countries, alcohol consumption is likely to increase. It is, therefore, hypothesized that PDS may be higher in high- and middle-income countries than in low-income countries. OECD records show that alcohol consumption is about twice the world average in OECD countries (OECD 2015). This reports further contends that, "When it is not the result of addiction, alcohol use is an individual choice, driven by social norms, with strong cultural connotations" (OECD 2015).

Acknowledging the evidence of association between the combined influence of binge patterns of drinking, the type of alcoholic beverages consumed, and the role of economic affluence on the harmful consequences of drinking, an attempt is made to use them as predictors of PDS. The WHO's indicator of PDS ranges from 1 (least risky drinking patten) to 5 (most risky drinking pattern). Since the PDS indicator represents ordered categories (that have a natural ordering), the present exercise uses an "ordinal" regression approach to analyze the PDS data of 88 countries. The ordered logit model, aka the proportional odds model (ologit/po), is recommended when the categories of response variables follow a natural rank ordering (Williams et al. 2016).

The purpose of applying ordinal regression on a cross-section of countries is to determine the direction of the relationship between each predictor and the ordinal nature of the categorical outcome (PDS in our example) (Chan 2005).

MODEL: ORDINAL LOGIT

If the response variable, y, is ordinal, we can take account of the ordering by use of cumulative probabilities, cumulative odds, and cumulative logits. Considering j ordered response categories, these can be defined as

Cumulative probabilities: $P(y \leq j) = P_1 + P_2 + ...P_j$

With three categories of response variable, the cumulative probabilities can be presented as

P(y = 1), P(y ≤ 2) = P(y = 1) + P(y = 2), P(y ≤ 3) =1.

The odds of response in category j or below is the ratio P(y ≤ j)/ P(y > j).

Cumulative odds: $ods(y \leq j) = \frac{P(y \leq j)}{P(y > j)} = \frac{P_1 + P_2 + ...P_i}{P_{i+1+}P_{i+2}....P_j}$

Cumulative Logits (logits of cumulative probabilities): $Logit(y \leq j) = Ln\left(\frac{P(Y \leq j)}{P(y > j)}\right)$

With j=3, the logits are (Agresti 2018)

$$Logit\ P(y \leq 1) = \log[\frac{P(y=1)}{P(y>1)}] = \log[\frac{P(y=1)}{P(y=2)+P(y=3)}]$$

$$Logit\ P(y \leq 2) = \log[\frac{P(y \leq 2)}{P(y>2)}] = \log[\frac{P(y=1)+P(y=2)}{P(y=3)}]$$

Each cumulative logit regards the response as binary by considering whether the response is at the low end or the high end of the scale (Agresti 2018)

If the slope coefficients are assumed to remain constant across j categories, we can avoid the problem of estimating a large number of coefficients. This assumption is known as a proportional odd model assumption, in which β ($logit\ slope$) coefficients are assumed to be the same across all cut-off (threshold) points. If we invoke this assumption, the cumulative logistic model for ordinal response data is simplified to

$$Logit\left(Y \le j\right) = \alpha_j + \beta_1 x_1 + \beta_2 x_2 + \ldots\ldots_+ \beta_p x_p \ldots\ldots \text{(iii)}$$

Where α_j denotes thresholds (intercepts), and β_1, β_2,----------β_p are slope coefficients. The above expression (iii) is the standard parametrization for the proportional odds model. In this parametrization, for an increasing value of X, a positive beta refers to higher odds of a lower ordered category.

This indicates that cumulative odds of the response in category j or below can be expressed as

$$Odds\left(Y \le j\right) = \exp\left(\alpha_j\right)\exp\left(\beta_1 x_1 + \beta_2 x_2 + \ldots\ldots_+ \beta_p x_p\right)$$

Some types of software, such as SPSS and STATA, use a minus sign before the coefficient for predictors[33]. This specification is given below in (iv), which differs from (iii).

$$= Logit\left[\left(P\left(y \le j\right)\right)\right] = \alpha_j + \left(-\beta_1 x_1 - \beta_2 x_2 --- \beta_p x_p\right) \text{-------- for j=1, 2, n-1-------------(iv)}$$

For j=3, each model (iv) describes two relationships: the effect of x on the odds that y≤1 instead of y>1, and the effect on the odds that y≤2 instead of y>2 (Agesti 2018). The model requires separate intercepts, α_j, for each cumulative probability.

In the above parameterization (iv), a positive value of β indicates that with increasing value for x, the odds of being above a given value of j (threshold point) increase. In other words, a positive coefficient indicates higher odds of moving to the next higher ordered category for higher values of x (higher x tends to occur with higher y) (Agesti 2018).[34]

---

33   SAS does not negate the signs before the logit coefficients in the equations (See Liu 2009).

34   Another way of saying this is: we are less likely to observe relatively low values (cumulative probabilities being lower with positive beta in $\left(\alpha_j - \beta x\right)$, and more likely to observe a higher value of y (Agesti 2004, P 4140).

The Estimated Model

The model used here to predict risky pattern of drinking is specified below :

Logit[p(PDS≤j)]=α_j -β_1 Spirit content -β_2 Relative Economic affluence,

where: (a) the response variable, PDS(termed as 'pattern of drinking score'), is an ordinal response variable with a score varying from 1 (least risky pattern) to 3(most risky drinking pattern); the spirit content (percentage) in alcohol is assumed to be a continuous predictor variable; (c) relative economic influence is a dichotomous predictor, comprising of two country groups: LLMICs (low- and lower-middle income countries)=1, and HUMICs (high- and upper-middle income countries)=2

The estimated results are reported below in Tables from 12a to 12e. The discussion below starts by examining the goodness-of-fit.

Assessing the goodness-of-fit

To assess the goodness of fit, we examine the information in Table 12a. From the table, we see that the difference between the two likelihoods (change in −2 log likelihood when independent variables are added to a model that contains only the intercept)—the chi-square—has an observed significance level of less than 0.001. This means that the model with additional predictor variables is a good fit, and we reject the null that the model with intercept only (without predictors) is as good as the model with the predictors. We can also say that the model with predictors has significantly better fit than the model with intercept only, $\chi^2(3) = 37.50$, p < .001

Table 12a: Ordinal Regression Output

Model	-2 Log Likelihood	Chi-Square	df	Sig.
Intercept Only	178.426			
Final	141.929	37.497	3	.000

Second, for goodness of fit, the statistics are intended to test whether the observed data are consistent with the fitted model. We start from the null hypothesis that the fit is good. If we do not reject this hypothesis (i.e., if the p-value is large), then we conclude that the data and the model predictions are similar and that we have a good model.[35] If the model fits well,

---

35   ReStore, National Centre for Research Methods, Using Statistical Regression Methods in Education

then the observed and expected cell counts are similar, the value of each statistic is small, and the observed significance level is large. In Table 12b, we see that the goodness-of-fit measures have large observed significance levels; therefore, it appears that the model fits.

Table 12b: Goodness of Fit

	Chi-Square	df	Sig.
Pearson	152.721	156	.559
Deviance	139.156	156	.829

Both the Pearson and deviance tests are non-significant ($\chi^2 (156)) = 152.72$, p = .56 and $\chi^2(156) = 139.16$, p = .83) suggesting good overall model fit.

Third, to evaluate the strength of the association in logit functions, the commonly used statistics are Cox and Snell R^2, Nagelkerke's R^2, and McFadden's R^2. In our example, the values of all the pseudo R^2 statistics are in the acceptable range and are not too low.

Table 12c: Pseudo R-Snell

	Chi-Square
Cox and Snell	.356
Nagelkerke	.401
McFadden	.201

Test of Parallel Lines (Proportional Odds)

When we fit an ordinal regression, we assume that the relationships between the independent variables and the logits are the same for all the logits. The test of parallel lines is used to assess the assumption of proportional odds–that is, the same slope coefficient, β_i across all logit functions. From Table 12d, it is seen that the observed significance level is large (>0.05), which means we do not have sufficient evidence to reject the parallelism hypothesis. The parallel model is adequate.

Research, Module 5. http://www.restore. ac.uk/srme/www/fac/soc/wie/research-new/srme/modules/.

Table 12d: Test of Parallel Lines

Model	-2 Log Likelihood	Chi-Square	df	Sig.
Null Hypothesis	141.929			
General	139.37	2.559	2	.278

Table 12e: Parameter Estimates

	Estimate	Std. Error	Wald	df	Sig.	Lower Bound	Upper Bound
[Least Risky =1]	1.216	0.524	5.378	1	.020	.188	2.243
[Moderately Risky=2]	3.195	0.631	25.650	1	.000	1.958	4.431
Covariate: Percentage of Spirit content in Alcohol Factor: Dummy for LLMICs=1	.053	0.017	9.791	1	.002	.020	.086
Dummy for HHMICS=2	1.679	0.494	11.544	1	.001	.710	2.647
	0			0			

Note: PDS is classified here into 3 categories-1,2,3.

EXAMINING THE COEFFICIENTS

The Table 12e presents the parameter (beta) estimates, the standard error (S.E.), the Wald statistic, the significance level. The threshold coefficients are not usually interpreted individually. They are the intercepts, specifically the cut off points for the response variable to be predicted into higher category. The cut-off points in the ordered logit model are explained below.

In ordered logit model there is an observed ordinal variable, Y which is a function of another variable unmeasured latent variable Y.* This latent variable has various threshold points, κ. In our example, for j=3(Least risky pattern, moderately risky pattern and highly risky pattern), we have the following responses categories of Y(Williams & Quiroz 2019) :

$Y=1$ if Y^* is $\leq \kappa_1$

$Y=2$ if $\kappa_1 \leq Y^*$ is $\leq \kappa_2$

$Y=3$ if $\kappa_2 \leq Y^*$ is $\leq \kappa_3$

Three cut off points ae used here to differentiate adjacent categories of risky pattern of drinking. The threshold estimate [less risky pattern = PDS = 1.00] is the cutoff value between low and moderately risky, and the threshold estimate for [moderately risky = PDS = 2.00] represents the cutoff value between moderately and highly risky patterns of drinking.

The p-values of both the predictors are shown in the sixth column of table 12e. The test results reveal that both the variables have p-value < 0.005, indicating these variables have significant effect on the response variable.

The magnitude of the effect of predictors of PDS (response variable) can be described by estimated odd ratios (Bender and Grouven 1997). With j=3 and two predictors, the proportional odd(PO) model can be rewritten as (Liu 2009):

$Logit\left[p\left(Y \leq 3 \,|\, x\right)\right] = \alpha_j + \left(\beta_1 x_1 - \beta_2 x_2 \right)$ .... (v)

The predicted logit for LLMICs of being at or below level 1, $Logit\left[p\left(Y \leq 1 \,|\, x\right)\right]$ =1.216-1.679*(1)= -0.463.

The predicted logit for HUMICs at or below level 1, $Logit\left[p\left(Y \leq 1 \,|\, x\right)\right]$ =1.216-0*(2)=1.216, since $\beta_2 = 0$ for HUMICs. From the details provided in table 13, we obtain odd ratio of LLMICs versus HUMICs=5.36. This odd ratio is same across other thresholds(See 2nd column in table 13). This ratio can also be obtained by exponentiating β_2 (=exp(1.679)=5.36), which indicates the odds $P(PDS > j)/PDS \leq j$) for LLMICS of being above any category versus being at or below that category to be 5.36 times the odds for HMICs. That means, with increase in the value of predictor, x_2 by one unit(which means as LLMICS progress to higher category, the positive $\hat{\beta}_2$ =1.679 indicates LLMICs are likely to shift to more risky pattern of drinking(y>j rather than y≤j).(Agresti 2018, P475-476). For our continuous variable indicator, we observe that every unit increase in spirit contents, the odds of high risk versus the combined moderate and low risk categories are 1.0544(=exp(0.053) times greater, given the other variable(X_2) is held constant in the model.

For our continuous variable indicator, we observe that every unit increase in spirit contents, the odds of high risk versus the combined moderate and low risk categories are 1.0544(=exp(0.053) times greater, given the other variable(X_2) is held constant in the model.

TABLE 13: Predicted cumulative logits, estimated odds of being at or below category j for LLMICs and HUMICs

LLMICs	Low Risk Drinking Pattern [Y=1]	Moderately Risky Drinking Pattern [Y=2]
Cumulative Logit	$-0.463(=1.216-\beta_2)$	$1.516(=3.195-\beta_2)$
Cumulative Odd(Exp(Cum logit)	0.629	4.55
Cumulative Proportions[1/(1+exp(Cum logit)]	0.6137	0.18
HUMIC(Reference Category)		
Cumulative Logit	1.216	3.195
Cumulative Odd(Exp(Cum logit)	3.37	24.41
Cumulative Proportions[1/(1+exp(Cum logit)]	0.228	0.039
Odd Ratios(LLMICs /HHMICs	3.37/0.629=5.36	24.41/4.55=5.36

Note: $\beta_2 =1.679$

UNIVERSAL PREVENTION, EARLY INTERVENTION, AND HARM-REDUCTION POLICIES

U nderage drinking has been labeled as an endemic problem that requires significant prevention-related interventions. Scientific evidence accumulated over the past three decades and the positive effects and outcomes of several prevention programs in developed countries show that all alcohol-attributable burdens are, in principle, completely avoidable and could be prevented in a relatively short time frame (WHO 2009, Ch. 4; Rehm and Imtiaz 2016).

PREVENTION INTERVENTIONS AND HARM REDUCTION PROGRAMS

Prevention efforts have been considered especially important for young people, who constitute a group that is at particular risk for the consequences of alcohol use (National Institute on Alcohol Abuse and Alcoholism; US Alcohol Alert). Communities, schools, and workplaces provide essential venues for reaching risky adolescent drinkers with prevention messages and strategies. While preventive strategies have a great deal of appeal and provide essential measures to prevent easy access to alcohol by vulnerable and high-risk groups, other policy interventions and more targeted harm-reduction approaches are still needed to deal with high-risk drinking among adolescents. Without proactive policies, risky patterns of drinking among teenagers and young adults will continue to result in considerable personal and societal suffering around the world. Misuse of alcohol and drug use is causing a high the disease burden and deaths for young people in developed nations (Toumbourouet al 2007). To contain the disease burden and adverse social consequences, epidemiologists and public health officials have suggested adding harm-reduction strategies, along with population-based prevention (abstinence) policies. An emerging consensus acknowledges that when dealing with problematic drinkers, harm-minimization programs may work at least as well as the prevention programs that aim to achieve the complete elimination of alcohol use (Marlatt and Witkiewitz 2002). An effective method of dealing with underage drinking, thus, requires an integrated and broad-based approach that combines regulatory-prevention, early-intervention, and harm-reduction programs (Toumbourou et al 2007).

Section 4.1 deals with prevention policies(universal, selective and indicated). Table 14 in this subsection 4.1 lists widely researched preventive measures. Risk and protective framework suggests prevention interventions aim to prevent onset of harmful patterns in settings such as vulnerable families, schools, and communities. Table 15 briefly summarizes interventions that aim both at prevention and harms reduction for adolescents and youth. Harm reduction approach is introduced in section 4.2.

4.1 PREVENTION STRATEGIES FOR THE UNDERAGE POPULATION

Research studies have revealed that physiological changes (such as physical growth, brain development, and puberty) and psychological and social changes (such as an evolving sense of self, the formation of more mature relationships with friends, and the transition from middle to high school) are critical transitional periods that need to be monitored and specifically targeted in order to design more effective measures for preventing or treating underage drinking (National Institute on Alcohol Abuse and Alcoholism [NIAAA] 2009). Early adolescence (11–14 years) is considered a very sensitive and vulnerable period of development during which the initiation of alcohol use is particularly harmful, warranting an urgent and priority response (Guttmannova et al. 2011). Even the period from 16 to 20 years of age, late adolescence, is known as a period of extensive and rapid transition in virtually every domain of life functioning (Brown et al 2008).

Teenage alcohol use has been found to be a well-known correlate of school failure and reduced educational attainment. Heavy alcohol use in adolescence diminishes educational attainment by affecting brain structure, brain functioning, and neuropsychological performance (Staff et al. 2008). Investigating the long-term impact of heavy alcohol use at age 16 on educational qualifications in adulthood, Staff et al. (2008) found evidence that heavy teenage alcohol use and disadvantaged social origins combined to diminish male educational attainment. Guo et al. (2001) showed that "at the early age of ten, efforts that prevent and reduce delinquency, prevent and reduce a child's association with and bonding to antisocial and alcohol-using peers and prevent children from developing favorable attitudes toward alcohol use may also reduce the risk of alcohol abuse and dependence in young adulthood" (p. 760). For the early prevention, intervention, and management of alcohol-related problems, a six-country WHO collaborative project, "The Alcohol Use Disorders Identification Test (AUDIT)," has been developed. It is a screening instrument for hazardous and harmful alcohol consumption (Saunders et al. 1993). According to this test, a score of eight or more refers to hazardous or harmful alcohol use.

Advances in psychosocial research and neuroscience have provided new avenues for the prevention of substance abuse at the individual and community levels (Medina-Mora 2005). Various multicomponent prevention programs have been developed, taking into consideration multiple antecedents of adolescent substance abuse (Hawkins et al. 2002), These include school-based strategies (e.g., educational programs, social skills, and lifestyle education), programs involving the adolescents' families, and national laws and policies (e.g., raising the minimum legal drinking age [MLDA] and reducing the economic availability of alcohol),that include simultaneously limiting commercial access to alcohol and the promotion of its use (Kumro et al. 2002; Strøm et al. 2014; Harding et al. 2016; Holder 2000; Nation et al. 2003). Prevention strategies that target salient risk and protective factors at all levels—individual, family, and community—hold great promise (Hawkins et al. 2002; Bränström et al. 2008; Griffin and Botvin 2010). These strategies are discussed in the following subsection

Universal, Selective and Indicated Interventions

The IOM (2009) has described three categories of prevention intervention: universal, selective, and indicated. Universal interventions target all members of a given population (for instance, all underage people); selective interventions are aimed at a subgroup that is determined to be at high risk of substance use (for instance, children with alcoholic parents, low-income/single-parent families, and students at risk of dropping out of school [Durlak and Wells 1997]); while indicated interventions are targeted at individuals who are already using substances but have not developed an SUD (i.e., children with early signs of maladjustment).

4.1.1 UNIVERSAL PRIMARY INTERVENTIONS

Population-based universal primary intervention is a class of prevention interventions that is widely researched, is evidence-based, is grounded on the developmental perspective, and attempts to minimize drinking risks before the onset of symptoms.[36] Primary interventions aim at reducing or eliminating risk factors and enhancing protective factors

---

36 Primary prevention has been classified into universal, selective, and indicated, according to the level of risk of using substances.

in individuals and their environments during their critical life stages (Hawkins, Catalano, and Arthur 2002). Risk factors, whether proximal or distant, can be moderated through primary intervention approaches.[37] Universal prevention policies are likely to reach most or all of the population (for example, school-based interventions, such as social and emotional learning, are likely to reach all students). These policies have the potential to delay early use and stop the progression from use to problematic use or to an SUD (including its severest form—addiction), all of which are associated with costly individual, social, and public health consequences (US Department of Health and Human Services [HHS], Office of the Surgeon General, Facing Addiction in America 2016).

Universal primary population-based interventions fall into three categories: (A) structural (e.g., laws and macro-level regulatory, price, and taxation policies),[38] (B) school-based, family-based, and surrounding neighborhood–based policies (Stockings et al. 2016), and (C) universal early childhood development programs. From the neuroscience perspective, a strict and prudent macro-level focus on regulatory policies is hypothesized to act as effective as risk-prevention programs. Second, individual-focused interventions (which seek to change knowledge, expectations, attitudes, intentions, motivations, and skills to resist the surrounding pro-drinking influences and opportunities (NIAAA 2006)) include school- and family-based prevention programs, although such interventions may also act at the environmental level. "Nurturing care" during the early childhood development years, that encompass prenatal period through age 8, helps to protect infants and children from the negative impact of stress and adversity. Public funded universal early child-hood development programs can play a very significant role strong foundations for a healthy developmental trajectory. All these population-based universal interventions are explained below in this subsection 4.1.1.

A. MACRO-LEVEL REGULATIONS AND LAWS RESTRICTING ACCESS TO ALCOHOL

Hawkins et al. (1992) argue that individuals and groups exist within social contexts, which consist of social values and myriad cultural structures. At the societal level, lax regulations about the accessibility of alcohol and drugs to adolescents and wider

---

37 Universal, selective, and indicated preventive interventions are included within primary prevention in the public health classification (WHO 2004). Prevention of Mental Disorders: Effective Interventions and Policy Options, Summary Report.

38 Such macro-level policies involve taking into account several alcohol-related concerns: (i) setting the real price of alcoholic beverages so that it reflects ethanol content, (ii) ensuring prices do not fall too low and are adjusted in accordance with the cost-of-living index, (iii) regulating the number of licensed premises (e.g., through government alcohol monopolies), (iv) administrating random breath testing, and (v) legislating a low legal blood-alcohol concentration limit for drivers (WHO 2010b, 2014a).

promotion and publicity heighten the risks of adolescents' taking a positive view of liquor consumption. Schulenberg et al. (2002) highlighted the important role of macro-level interventions, such as changing social norms (e.g., acceptability of heavy drinking), altering laws and penalties for violations (e.g., legislative changes regarding parental notification), changing marketing regulations, and providing substance-free housing. The WHO (2010) lists five specific macro-environmental interventions for limiting the chances of transitioning to the harmful use of alcohol:

1. increase prices and excise taxes;
2. limit availability, either through sales regulations that restrict consumer groups or through sales regulations that restrict how alcohol is sold (Hawkins et al. 1992);
3. ban advertising and regulate mass media (Zucker et al. 2008);
4. enforce drunk-driving laws (e.g., breath testing); and
5. offer brief advice against hazardous drinking.

Of these, the first three policies are considered "best buys," as their implementation is cheap, feasible, and culturally acceptable. Minimum age drinking laws can reduce the rate of underage drinking. Legal and supply restrictions influence the availability during prescribed hours and to eligible populations, as do price levels. Availability and social acceptability exert a powerful influence that increases the likelihood of drug use. Research studies support the above recommendations.

Certain liberal alcohol availability policies—such as the privatization of retail sales (off-premises retail sales), increase in the density of alcohol outlets, and increased sale hours and days—increase access to alcohol and cause excessive alcohol consumption (Popova et al. 2009; Hahn et al. 2010; Gruenewald 2011). Using cross-sectional survey and geospatial data with university campus- and individual-level analyses, Kypri et al. (2008) suggested that increasing alcohol-outlet density, and particularly off-licenses, increases alcohol-related harm among university students. On the basis of their review of several studies, Campbell et al. (2009) concluded that greater alcohol-outlet density was associated with increased alcohol consumption and related damage, including medical harm, crime, and violence. In their view, reduced alcohol-outlet density can be an effective means of controlling excessive alcohol consumption and harm.

Cross-sectional samples from the Russian Longitudinal Monitoring Survey revealed a significant positive correlation between the amount of alcohol consumed and the number of hours of allowed alcohol sales when other factors were controlled for (Kolosnitsyna, Sitdikov, and Khorkina 2014). In their global analysis, Chisholm et al. (2018) supported the "best buys" for alcohol control in that they have found evidence that pricing policies and restrictions on alcohol availability and marketing continued to represent a highly cost-effective use of resources more than a decade after their introduction. Russia is cited as one of the countries that experienced marked changes in both alcohol use and the alcohol-attributable burden of disease as a result of implementing the WHO's so-called "best buys" (recommended interventions such as taxation, availability restrictions, and a ban on marketing) and minimum pricing (Manthey et al. 2019).

It is, however, contended that the abovementioned macro-level preventive regulations cannot yield significant positive outcomes if adopted in isolation from the surrounding social environment. One significant challenge is to develop and implement prevention strategies that help to develop resiliency in youth and to protect them from potentially negative and harmful aspects of their individual interpersonal environments, such as their families, schools, and communities. Using the social development model (SDM), Guo et al. (2001) examined the role of sociodemographic variables along with socio-environmental norms influencing alcohol abuse and dependence in young adults. Guo et al. (2001) found that at ages 10, 14, and 16, individual, family, peer, school, and community factors predicted alcohol abuse and dependence in early adulthood. Their findings highlight the important influence of the following protective factors: early formation and maintenance of strong bonds to school, maintenance of close parental monitoring and clear family rules for behavior, provision of appropriate parental rewards for children's good behavior, enhancement of refusal skills, and promotion of pro-social beliefs. Many of these predictors have also been found to be important explanatory factors in other studies of problem behavior among youth, such as early high school dropout rates, violence, and gang membership (Guo et al. 2001, p. 760).

B. INTERVENTIONS TO ADDRESS INDIVIDUALS' RISK AND INTERPERSONAL ENVIRONMENTAL FACTORS

Individuals and their interpersonal environments—families, classrooms, and peer groups—are risk factors for adolescents' substance abuse (Hawkins et al. 1992). Individual risk factors include, but are not limited to, physiological factors, early and persistent behavioral problems, academic failures, and a low degree of commitment to school. Longitudinal research has identified a substantial set of variables predicting teenage alcohol use. These variables include gender; socioeconomic background; non-intact family structure; parent's substance use; family conflict and low parental monitoring; difficult child temperament, aggressiveness, and negative affect; low academic motivation, aspirations, and school grades; and associations with deviant peers (Staff et al. 2008). Using evidence from their cross-sectional study on students in grades seven through twelve, Resnick et al. (1997) reported that students with a high frequency of alcohol use had lower grade point averages and lower self-esteem than students in the same grades who did not use alcohol. Hawkins et al. (1992) suggested the SDM, which asserts that children learn pro-social and antisocial behaviors from socializing agents in the contexts of family, school, peer groups, and religious and other community institutions (Hawkins and Weis 1985; Catalano and Hawkins 1996).

Failure to develop compliance in the early years may seriously compromise later social functioning at school and with peers. Both early drinking and alcoholism have been linked to personality characteristics, such as strong tendencies to act impulsively and to seek out new experiences and sensations (NIAAA 2003). One form of impulsivity—sensation seeking and risk taking (particularly in the presence of peers)—rises dramatically during adolescence and increases risks to healthy development (Romer 2010). Some evidence indicates that genetic factors may contribute to the relationship between early drinking and subsequent alcoholism (NIAAA 2003).

According to Masten and Coatsworth (1998), self-regulation is an important capability that is required for the development of social compliance. Problems in academic achievement have been linked to problems of self-regulation, especially in regard to attention and impulsive behavior, as well as antisocial behavior (Masten and Coatsworth 1998). These researchers further argue that self-regulation skills account, at least in part, for the generally recognized ability of IQ scores to accurately predict individual competence and resilience. Moreover, children who have trouble directing their attention or controlling their impulses may not do well on IQ tests or in the classroom generally, may fail to comply with rules, and may have problems in getting along well with their peers.

In a review of existing programs on positive youth development, Catalano et al. (2004) examined 77 programs and identified[39] 25 as successful. In the successful programs, 14 positive youth-development constructs were covered in the interventions. These 14 positive constructs relate to the following areas:

1. Social bonding
2. Social competence
3. Emotional competence
4. Cognitive competence
5. Behavioral competence
6. Moral competence
7. Self-efficacy
8. Pro-social norms
9. Resilience
10. Self-determination
11. Beliefs in the future

---

39 An American Addiction Centers Resource, Peer Pressure of teen drinking, Alcohol.org, https://www.alcohol.org/teens/peer-pressure-drinking/.

12. Clear and positive identity
13. Pro-social involvement
14. Positive behavior

The socio-environmental factors that are associated with improvements in youth development include school, family, peer, and community resources. These social domains of influence are discussed below. Adolescence is a period of formative years that require multiple coordinate actions across several social domains. Guo et al 2001), among others, suggest actions that include the following key elements: establishing strong bonds to school early and maintaining them, maintaining close parental monitoring and clear family rules for behavior, providing appropriate parental rewards for children's good behavior, enhancing refusal skills, and promoting pro-social beliefs. The following evidence-based interventions that deal with the multiple risk and protective factors are commonly suggested.

FAMILY-BASED INTERVENTIONS

The family plays a key role in both preventing and intervening in substance use and misuse through reducing risk and/or encouraging and promoting protection and resilience (Velleman, Templeton, and Copello 2005). Stable and supportive family structures buffer the impact of stress and promote resilience in the child. Without such stability and support, the impact of other risk factors can be intensified (Leyton and Stewart 2014). Medical research indicates that a person faces a higher risk of addiction if there is a family history of addiction. Alcohol expectancies have been shown to be a genetically influenced characteristic, having a heritability of between 0.4 and 0.6 (Courtney and Polich 2009).

Belcher and Shinitzky (1998) observed that the earliest influence to smoke, drink alcohol, or use drugs may come from the family. Evidence from US studies indicates that around 57% of current underage drinkers reported family and friends as the source of the alcohol they consumed (SAMHSA 2019). Parental interventions, such as monitoring the child's behavior and setting clear rules against drinking, are advocated for reducing the likelihood of underage drinking. Multiple studies have revealed that more social and assertive children have parents with authoritative parenting styles who enforce rules, provide a nourishing parental environment, respond to and show respect for children as independent and rational beings, promote positive family relationships, and exhibit involvement and attachment (Hawkins et al. 1992). Cohen's study provides evidence that parenting styles and adolescents' perceptions of them are associated with child achievement and substance use.

Healthy child-rearing methods (characterized by emotional support and love, the implementation of rules and consequences that regulate and control behavioral problems, and supportive responsiveness) are contemplated to reduce the conduct problems and improve the school performance of those who demonstrate a low, or complete lack of, commitment to school and their education (Hawkins et al. 1992; Masten and Coatsworth 1998). A high level of connectedness to parents and family members is associated with less frequent use of alcohol among students (Resnick et al. 1997).

SCHOOL-BASED PROGRAMS

Schools are another important and essential setting for interventions aimed at preventing alcohol use and abuse among adolescents (Stigler, Neusel, and Perry 2011). For a teenager, risky times occur when they enter school. Later, when they transition from elementary to middle school, they often experience new academic and social situations, such as learning to get along with a wider group of peers. When they enter high school, teens may encounter greater availability of drugs, association with drug-abusing peers, and social activities in which drugs are used. Epidemiological surveys in the US, such as the National Epidemiologic Survey on Alcohol and Related Conditions and the National Survey of Drug Use and Health, have indicated that the prevalence of alcohol dependence is highest in late adolescence (ages 18–20) and early young adulthood (ages 21–24), with rates declining thereafter (Windle and Zucker 2010). Within these age groups, those at highest risk of belonging to heavier-drinking subgroups tend to be those who are male, who often do not live with two biological parents, and whose parents are heavy alcohol users who exhibit obvious symptoms of alcoholism and/or antisocial personality (Maggs and Schuleberg 2004/2005). Prevention programs aimed at the general population at key transition points can produce beneficial effects even among high-risk families and children (NIDA 2003).

In developed nations, universal schooling provides a comprehensive representation of student populations, offering the potential to monitor early-use patterns in younger age groups (Toumbourou et al. 2007). School-based efforts are extremely efficient in that they offer easy access to large numbers of students. School-based alcohol interventions are designed to reduce risk factors for early alcohol use, primarily at the individual level (e.g., by enhancing students' knowledge and skills), although the most successful school-based programs also address social and environmental risk factors (e.g., alcohol-related cultural norms). High levels of school connectedness have been found to be associated with less frequent use of alcohol by adolescent students (Resnick et al. 1997).

Teachers can improve children's attitudes toward school, behavior at school, and academic achievement through the use of effective methods of instruction and management. Classroom-based skills training (through instruction, modeling, and role playing) for adolescents in grades five through ten, and particularly grades six and seven, has been recommended to teach students how to resist social influences and peer pressure to use drugs (Hawkins et al. 1992). In addition, cooperative learning strategies in elementary and middle schools, academic tutoring of low achievers, and organizational changes in schools (curriculum restructuring, increased opportunity for student involvement, changes in school discipline procedures, and greater school–faculty–community integration) have been found to greatly enhance students' academic performance and reduce dropout rates (Hawkins et al. 1992).

Training teachers to teach and manage their classrooms in ways that promote bonding to school, training parents to manage their families in ways that promote bonding to family and school, and providing children with training in skills for social interaction are expected to have positive effects on children's attitudes toward school, their behavior at school, and their academic achievement (Hawkins et al. 1992). Maggs and Schulenburg (2004/2005) found that drug use prevention programs in middle schools would be appropriate for those subgroups experiencing the early onset of substance use that predicts ongoing heavier use. School-based programs targeting individual-level factors (i.e., curricula targeted at preventing alcohol, tobacco, or marijuana use) may need to be combined with extracurricular activities, family attention and involvement, and policy strategies that help change the overall social and cultural environment in which young people live, in order to create sustained decreases in alcohol consumption among youth (Komro and Toomey 2002).

Table 14: Risk and Protective Factors for Adolescents*

Domain	Risk Factors	Protective Factors
Individual	lack of social bonding; pro-attitude to drugs; antisocial, violent, and early aggressive behavior; academic failure (dropout); affiliation with deviant peers; poor coping skills; lack of behavioral control; low religiosity; susceptibility to negative peer influence; early onset of drinking; genetic predictors	resilient temperament; participation in extracurricular activities (sports, regular exercise, volunteer social work, and hobbies); success in school performance; positive social orientation; positive relationships; pro-social attitude; healthy beliefs; beliefs in religious activities

Family	family history of alcoholism; disorganized family; chaotic home environment; lack of mutual attachment and poor nurturing; low level of authoritative parenting; lack of parental supervision; parental permissibility of alcohol use; unclear rules; parental conflict (divorce)	healthy parenting; positive bonding among family members; emotionally supportive family environment; positive involvement of parents in educational activities; authoritative parenting
School	access to drugs and weapons; violence in schools, bullying, and delinquent peer culture; poor social support of students; poor administration and management practices; school disengagement (skipping school); disaffection from school (as expressed in truancy)	opportunities for youth participation in extracurricular activities; substance-use education in schools; social-competence training addressing emotional resilience; clear standards and rules against bullying; safe and healthy environment; training in social skills; cooperative learning; interactive teaching
Peers	affiliation with friends who engage in risky behavior; friends' alcohol/substance use in schools	authoritative parental monitoring; open communication between parents and adolescents/youth; school education to promote self-esteem and build resilience skills; parents' role in promoting academic competence
Community	easy availability of drugs for underage students; community norms favoring substance abuse; community disorganization; poverty; poor regulatory environment; resource barriers to early treatment; public health coverage gaps	strong regulations against access to alcohol; early childhood development support; increased opportunities for youth participation in community activities; SBIRT programs; affordable early and quality treatment

Sources: *Adapted from Sloboda and David (1997); Hawkins et al. (1992); Windle and Zucker (2010); Belcher HM and Shinitzky HE (1998); Patrick and Schulenberg (2014); Jessor et al. (2006); Prinstein et al. (2001); MTF (2015); and SAMHSA (2016)

ADDRESSING PEER PRESSURE

A young person's social identity is often molded by his or her social group and desire to fit in and be part of the "in crowd" (Alcohol Org. Editorial Staff 2019).[40] The perception that "everyone is doing it" can also influence teenagers to consume alcohol so that they will be part of the crowd. For many teenagers, adolescence is a phase of experimentation, and the most important reference group in this regard is their peers (Steketee et al. 2013). This report further adds that because drinking is a largely social phenomenon, and given that adolescents often drink as a way to become integrated into groups and gain status, it should come as no surprise that a more peer-oriented lifestyle is strongly associated with alcohol use. It is said that adolescents who are in the company of friends consume alcohol mostly for social and enhancement motives during gatherings. A report by the NIAA (2003) suggests that the most reliable predictor of a youth's drinking behavior is the drinking behavior of his or her friends. Friends' alcohol use in high school predicted both concurrent and future trajectories of binge drinking (Patrick and Schulenberg 2014). The frequency of evenings out with friends (unsupervised by adults) was associated with more alcohol and other drug use (Patrick and Schulenberg 2014).

The linkages between peers' and adolescents' health-risk behaviors may be compounded by factors in the family domain, such as low levels of support from family, family dysfunction (disorganized families), increased susceptibility to negative peer influence, and a higher likelihood of imitating the risk behavior of friends. Peer and parental influences may function together in impacting adolescent friendship choices and drinking behavior (Wang et al. 2015). These authors' findings suggest that while adolescents' peer relationships were central to their lives, parents still had an influence on both adolescent alcohol use and friendship choices. Investigations have demonstrated that alcohol use by adolescents' friends, for instance, is substantially associated with adolescents' alcohol use (see Hawkins, Catalano, and Miller 1992). Moreover, there is some evidence to suggest that friends' risk behavior may be causal; that is, affiliation with risky peers is related to increases in adolescents' risk behavior over time (Prinstein et al. 2001).

C. UNIVERSAL PUBLICLY FUNDED EARLY-CHILDHOOD PROGRAMS

Early Childhood Phase: The science of early brain development makes a compelling case for investment in early childhood.[41] Although the brain continues to develop and change

---

40   Peer Pressure of Teen Drinking, Alcohol.Org

41   Early childhood development covers children aged zero to eight years (WHO, United Nations Children's Fund, World Bank Group 2018) and includes the following developmental periods: (i) prenatal period; (ii) infancy

into adulthood, the period during pregnancy and the first three years after birth lay down critical elements of health, well-being, and productivity, which last throughout childhood, adolescence, and adulthood (WHO, United Nations Children's Fund, World Bank Group 2018). The early years of life are the period of maximum brain growth and the formation of emotional regulatory patterns that affect later mental health outcomes (Kieling et al. 2011). Synaptic plasticity makes early childhood extremely sensitive to experiences and environmental influences (including family interactions and social contexts) that may either act as risk factors for later drug use and related problems or help protect against these risks (NIDA 2016, March). One area of the brain that is still maturing during adolescence is the prefrontal cortex,[42] which puts teenagers at increased risk for poor decisions (NIDA 2018, August). Early childhood development programs establish the basis for how a child forms social connection with others. Interactions between a child and his or her caregivers build the foundation for bonding that is key to the development of the child's capacity for motivated behavior. The explosion of research in neurobiology clarifies that creating the right conditions for early childhood development is likely to be more effective and less costly than addressing problems at a later age (The Science of Early Childhood Development 2007).

The essential ingredients of an effective childhood development program include making provisions for a stable home environment, adequate nutrition, physical and cognitive stimulation, warm and supportive parenting, and good classroom management in the early years of a child's life (prenatal through age eight) (NIDA 2016). These support programs have the potential to lead the child to develop strong self-regulation (i.e., emotional and behavioral control) and other qualities that delay the initiation and decrease the use of drugs when the child reaches adolescence (NIDA 2016). One underlying feature of early-childhood programs is that nurturing care initiatives ought to start even before the child is born. Nurturing care is considered necessary not only for children from families and communities with low income and low education levels but for all babies (WHO, United Nations Children's Fund, World Bank Group 2018).

Nurturing Care: Preventive and Promotive Interventions

Young children's healthy development depends on nurturing care—care that ensures health, nutrition, responsive caregiving, safety and security, and early learning (Lancet 2016;

---

and toddlerhood (birth to three years); (iii) preschool (ages three to six); and (iv) transition to school (ages six through eight) (NIDA 2016).

42   This part of the brain enables us to assess situations, make sound decisions, and keep our emotions and desires under control (NIDA, 2018 August): Research Report Series. Comorbidity: Addiction and other Mental Illness

Black et al. 2017; Britto et al. 2017). There are many preventive and promotive interventions to improve nurturing care between pregnancy and age three (WHO, United Nations Children's Fund, World Bank Group 2018). Nurturing care starts before birth, when mothers and other caregivers can start talking and singing to the fetus. Nurturing care is important for at least two reasons: It promotes young children's development, and it protects them from the worst effects of adversity by lowering their stress levels and encouraging the formation of emotional and cognitive coping mechanisms. The care and protection of young children are shared responsibilities because the future of any society depends on its ability to foster the health and well-being of the next generation (Shonkoff et al. 2012). Publicly funded, center-based, comprehensive early childhood development programs are suggested as a community resource that promotes the well-being of young children (Anderson et al. 2003). Population-based early childhood protective strategies, grounded in the application of advances in neuroscience, molecular biology, and genomics, can be highly cost-effective and have long-lasting impacts (Shonkoff 2009; Hawkins et al. 2002).[43] To take advantage of exciting new discoveries at the intersection of the biological, behavioral, and social sciences, interdisciplinary teams comprising scientists, practitioners, and policy makers need to work together to design, implement, and evaluate innovative strategies for early care childhood programs (Shonkoff 2009). The interdisciplinary and science-based nature of early-childhood programs necessitates a public health approach that also emphasizes collective action.

4.1.2 SELECTIVE AND INDICATED PREVENTIONS

Epidemiological research has brought to the forefront ample evidence that the earlier people try alcohol or drugs, the more likely they are to develop a SUD. Children are reported to be particularly vulnerable to initiating or escalating their involvement in problematic behaviors, such as drug abuse, during the transitional stages to adulthood (Kaplow, et al. 2002). There is a strong rationale for such prevention strategies because alcohol use typically begins during adolescence and young adulthood and may have long-term consequences.

Early intervention is defined as a therapeutic strategy that combines the early detection of hazardous or harmful substance use and the treatment of those involved (Charlois 2010). Such interventions aim to reduce substance use, risky patterns of substance use, and the harm that might arise from use (Stockings et al. 2016). The early initiation of drinking is found to be related (significantly) to an array of antecedent risk factors, such as personality

---

43   Per the WHO (2002) report on prevention, primary prevention can further be classified into three categories: (i) universal prevention policies that target the general public or a whole population group, (ii) selective prevention policies that target individuals or subgroups of the population whose risk of developing a mental disorder is significantly higher than that of the rest of the population, and (iii) indicated prevention, targeting persons at high risk of mental disorders.

characteristics (e.g., mental health, externalizing behavior in adolescence and adolescent deviant behavior, and the smoking habit); truancy (missing and skipping classes); parental drinking (or poor family management practices); being male (including ethnic origin); having a network of friends who drink; attending college and university etc. (Merline, Jager, and Schulenberg 2008; Hawkins et al. 1997). Because failure to develop compliance in the early years of life may seriously compromise later social functioning at school and with peers, early detection and interventions are considered highly effective in reducing the disease burden and adverse social consequences.

Early intervention and harm-reduction approaches are suggested to complement regulatory and abstinence-only approaches. Ample evidence suggests that adolescents and young adults stand to clearly benefit from the early prevention of high-risk drinking behavior (Marlatt 2002). Harm-reduction interventions are needed to prevent problems by targeting risky contexts or patterns of use. According to Marlatt (2002), "Harm reduction offers a pragmatic and compassionate approach to the prevention and treatment of problem drinking that shifts the focus away from alcohol use itself to the consequences of harmful drinking behavior" (p. 880). Evidence suggests that rates of tobacco use, harmful alcohol use, and illicit drug use in young people can be reduced through the concerted application of a combination of regulatory, early-intervention, and harm-reduction approaches (Toumbourou et al. 2007). Table 15 lists the interventions used to address substance use among adolescents and young people.

Early intervention and prevention programs can be selective or indicated. While selective and indicated prevention strategies are more often consistent with harm reduction, the latter approach (not abstinence-only/or not zero-tolerance) needs separate discussion, as its prime focus is not on prevention. In recent years, harm-reduction approaches have emerged to offer alternatives to zero-tolerance interventions aimed at prevention, because a substantial minority of adolescents show heavy and harmful patterns of substance use (Toumbourou et al. 2007).

Selected Targeted Interventions for Family and Neighborhood Risk Factors

Children brought up in homes in which the parents or other relatives use alcohol or drugs, for example, face a higher risk of trying these substances and of developing a SUD (HHS 2016, Ch. 3). Children from substance-affected families are an important target group for preventive efforts (Bröning et al. 2012). These family-supported community/public health interventions can include home visits by volunteers during pregnancy, childhood development programs, public campaigns addressing addiction and behavioral changes, social support networks and rehabilitation programs, alcohol screening tests for early detection, brief interventions, and others. Evidence from interventions involving home visits during pregnancy and early infancy—to address factors such as maternal smoking, poor social support, parental skills, and early child–parent interactions—has demonstrated significant improvement of mental health in both mothers and newborns, less need for and use of health services, and long-term reductions in problem behaviors in the children after the age of 15 years (WHO 2004). Interventions for children from impoverished families to enhance cognitive functioning and language skills have improved cognitive development and have led to better school achievement and fewer conduct problems (WHO 2004). Community support programs (such as home visits and violence counseling) that aim to ameliorate sociodemographic factors should intervene as early as possible to prevent risks for an infant. Second, living in neighborhoods and attending schools where alcohol and drug use are common and associating with peers who use substances are also risk factors (HHS 2016, Ch. 3). The perspective of "development epidemiology" (a special variety of epidemiology dealing with child psychopathology)[44] underscores the need to pay attention to the timing of the onset of disorders. This viewpoint also acknowledges that relations between causes and outcomes vary across the span of development to be addressed (Patel et al. 2007; Costello and Angold 1995).

Selective prevention programs incorporate elements of motivational and cognitive behavioral theory for coping with negative internal states (Lammers et al. 2015). Evidence suggests that for youth with personality risk factors, selective brief, early intervention through a qualified counselor and co-facilitator has proven to be highly effective for the early onset of alcohol use and to produce effects in reducing binge drinking that are comparable to those of the most evidence-based universal programs (Sherry et al. 2012, pp. 147–208). Lammers et al. (2015) and Conrad et al. (2013) suggest selective personality-targeted prevention interventions for pupils of middle or junior high school age. Lammers et al. (2015) describe four personality profiles of substance users: sensation seeking, impulsivity, anxiety sensitivity, and negative thinking. In their proposal, personality-targeted selective interventions are delivered and administered by trained teachers, mentors, counselors, and educational specialists (Conrad et al. 2013).

Indicated Preventive Programs

Indicated prevention addresses identified individuals with minimal but detectable signs or symptoms that suggest a disorder (Charlois 2010). The EU definition locates early intervention between indicated prevention and treatment as a therapeutic intervention based on the identification and observation of individuals using drugs. One group that is typically in need of early intervention is people who binge drink (HHS, Office of the Surgeon General 2016). In their review studies on underage drinking in the UK, Healey et al. (2004) mentioned the effectiveness of interventions such as therapist-assisted motivational and behavioral change

---

44 It may be noted that epidemiology is a scientific method of understanding the development of disease. Developmental epidemiology can, therefore, be seen as concerned with the interaction between two developmental processes: of the organism (the child) and of the disease. (For the definition of development epidemiology, see Costello and Angold 1995).

counseling. Brief Alcohol Screening and Intervention of College Students (BASICS) has been implemented both as an indicated prevention approach, based on the results of a brief screen for at-risk drinking, and as a selective prevention approach implemented with at-risk groups (e.g., fraternity members) regardless of individual drinking levels. These authors suggest that in both contexts, BASICS has demonstrated efficacy in reducing alcohol use, negative consequences, or both in the college population (Neihbors et al. 2006). Although BASICS, which, as indicated, is a prevention program for college students, is not designed for students who are alcohol dependent, its goal is considered to motivate students to reduce their alcohol use in order to decrease the negative consequences of drinking (Griffin and Botvin 2010).

Table 15: Types of Prevention Programs and Harm-Reduction Approaches

Prevention Types	Salient Features
Population-based universal prevention programs (Structural, School-Based, and Family-Based Interventions)	**Structural:** macro-level policies regarding issues such as taxes and the price of alcoholic beverages, the setting of an MLDA, liability laws (criminal social host liability laws and civil social host liability laws), restrictions on marketing and other regulations to reduce access to alcohol or consumption at the population level, and public-awareness mass-media campaigns Policies Delivered at School: generic psychosocial and developmental prevention programs, such as life-skills training and good-behavior games; drug abuse resistance education; and anti-bullying policies
	Policies Delivered to Families and Parents: interventions focusing on parental skills building, improving parent–child communication and relationships, and encouraging parental monitoring and supervision
	Investment in Early Childhood: strong nurturing environment for all children
Early Intervention Preventive Strategies: identifying children and adolescents at risk of substance use	**Selective:** community-/school-/family-based programs that target and monitor individuals with a family history of SUDs and families living in poverty in drug-infested and crime-ridden neighborhoods; individuals facing risk factors, including personality traits such as impulsivity or anxiety sensitivity and academic failure; individuals associating with or vulnerable to peer pressure; individuals making the transition from school to post-secondary/college education.
	Indicated: home-visiting programs, such as interventions from trained professionals for pregnant women in low-income neighborhoods; hospital-based selective prevention programs; and ASSIST-linked brief interventions; screening and brief intervention in adolescence

Harm Reduction Approach : policies focusing on minimizing the harmful effects of substance use	Treatment interventions with moderation goals; pharmacological harm-reduction treatment; life-skills training programs (based, e.g., on the cognitive behavioral approach); School Health and Alcohol Harm Reduction Project in the US; drinking-safety education in Washington[45]; random roadside breath testing; monitoring of needle-exchange practices; strict enforcement of drinking laws; driver's license penalties

Sources: Stockings et al. (2016); Foxcroft and Tsertsvadze (2011); Slutske 2005;[46] US Department of HHS, Office of the Surgeon General, Facing Addiction in America: The Surgeon General's Report on Alcohol, Drugs, and Health. Washington, DC: HHS, November 2016, Ch. 3; Spoth et al. (1999); Marlatt and Witkiewitz (2002); Toumbourou et al. 200

Critical Review of Prevention Strategies: Benefits and Shortfalls

Many community prevention programs are being experimented in the US (see details in SAMHSA 2016, Ch. 3) and focus on the developmental perspective on underage alcohol use, starting from the early formative years (Zucker et al. 2008; Masten et al. 2009). Assessing the effectiveness of alcohol policy interventions has been a great challenge for academicians and policy makers. To arrive at the most promising policy interventions, researchers have employed an accounting framework for defining and comparing the costs and benefits of alcohol consumption from various prevention support programs. Policy makers and other stakeholders use cost–benefit analysis as an informative tool for decision-making. The table 16, reproduced from SAMHSA 2016 (Original source: Washington State Institute for Public Policy 2016), provides estimates of the benefits per dollar cost of prevention programs.

Table 16: Benefits per Dollar Cost of Evidenced-Based Interventions (2015–2016)

Prevention Programs	Benefits per Dollar Cost
Nurse–Family Partnership	$1.61
Raising Healthy Children/(SSDP)	$4.27
Good-Behavior Game	$64.18
Life-Skills Training	$17.25
Keepin' it REAL*	$11.79
Strengthening Families Program (Children Aged 10–14)	$5
Guiding Good Choices	$2.69

---

45   See more details in Marlatt and Witkiewitz (2002).

46   Slutske WS (2005). Alcohol Use Disorders Among US College Students and Their Non-College-Attending Peers. *Arch Gen Psychiatry.* 2005; 62(3): 321–327. doi:10.1001/archpsyc.62.3.321.

Positive Family Support/Family Check-Up	$0.62
Project Toward No Drug Abuse	$6.54
BASICS**	$17.61

Source: reproduced from SAMHSA (2016).
NOTE: * Keepin' it REAL is a multicultural, school-based substance use prevention program for students 12–14 years old.
**** Brief Alcohol Screening and Intervention of College Students**

Evaluating benefit-cost for Communities that Care (CTC), Kuklinski et al. (2015) found that CTC was a cost-beneficial program (the estimated cost–benefit ratio was over $8 returned per dollar invested) for preventing the initiation of delinquency, alcohol use, and tobacco use in children and adolescents community-wide through grade 12. Their study consisted of a five-year intervention phase from 2003 to 2008, followed by a five-year sustainability phase concluding in 2013. Among childhood development interventions for which such data are available, it has been found that savings range from $2.88 for every dollar invested (the Nurse–Family Partnership described in Research-Based Early Intervention Substance Abuse Prevention Programs) to as much as $25.92 (the Good-Behavior Game used in the Classroom-Centered Intervention) (NIDA 2016 March 9).

Despite evidence of the cost-effectiveness of selected prevention strategies and their implementation, the rates of alcohol consumption among the underage population remains a problematic concern for not only drinkers but also society. The following section presents a brief review of the challenges in bridging the gap between theoretical advancements in prevention science and the consistent adoption of evidence-based interventions on a required scale.

Even though primary prevention programs have demonstrated considerable effectiveness and include changes in the MLDA; reductions in acceptable legal limits for BAC while operating a motor vehicle; and decreasing availability and access to alcohol for underage individuals (Kelly-Weeder et al. 2011), the concentration of the harmful use of alcohol among teenagers and young adults has continued to be a problem of concern. Studies have found that alcohol prevention programs have fallen short of delivering their expected benefits and failed to deal with the complexity of underage drinking behavior. Below is a short description of the critical challenges.

Implementation Challenges of Prevention Policies

Notwithstanding the clear evidence of the contribution of alcohol to the global burden of disease and the related substantial economic costs, the attention being paid to controlling alcohol consumption continues to be inadequate and sporadic in most countries (Gallimberti et al. 2011). It is alleged that most countries have no official guidelines for discouraging HED, but many have ongoing debates with a view to issuing guidelines in the near future (OECD 2015). Expressing concern about underage drinking in the US, Catalano (2018) found that prevention approaches that do not work or that have not been evaluated were more widely used than those that have been shown to be effective. Public regulations and market intervention policies that prevent harm are being overridden by the vested interests of the alcohol industry. Several factors interfere with the evidence-based prevention strategies used to reduce underage drinking; these include corporate lobbying to promote business interests, problems enforcing laws by local authorities, and inconsistent policies in different states (provinces) in a country, to mention just a few. As pointed out earlier, a substantial part of alcohol industry revenue (48.9% of consumer expenditure on alcohol consumption) comes from underage drinking and excessive drinking by adults; therefore, it is not in the financial interest of the industry to support public health strategies that aim to reduce excessive and underage drinking (Foster et al. 2003).

Corporate Lobbying Concerns: Corporate lobbying presents formidable challenges for public policies worldwide and disrupts evidence-based policy interventions by influencing marketing regulations (Casswell 2013; McCambridge et al. 2014; Moodie et al. 2013; Savell et al. 2016; Miller and Harkins 2010; Yoon and Lam 2013; Hawkins et al. 2018). Common strategies used by corporations to undermine effective public health policies and programs include the industry's capture of public policy[47] by biasing research findings, co-opting policy makers and health professionals, lobbying politicians and public officials to oppose public regulation, encouraging voters to oppose public regulations (Moodie et al. 2013), taking a weak regulatory approach toward alcohol products (Hawkins et al. 2018), misrepresenting corporate social responsibility practices in order to promote the industry's self-interest (Yoon and Lam 2013), and claiming that industry is responsible and self-regulation is effective (Savell et al. 2015; Moodie et al. 2013; Bakke and Endal 2010). In their review of 17 studies, Savell, Fooks, and Gilmore (2016) identified strategies that the alcohol industry uses to influence marketing regulations, including the promotion of self-regulation and the dissemination of information disputing evidence of the effectiveness of statutory regulations. According to Moodie et al. (2013, p. 6), "Industry-operated, voluntary self-regulation is the default approach of many governments and the UN, and the preferred approach of industry. This threatens alcohol laws towards achieving national health goals."

Evidence shows that the alcohol oligopolies in many countries permit oligopoly profit taking, which in turn facilitates higher marketing spending (Esser and Jernigan 2018). Comparing corporate control of tobacco versus alcohol products, Hawkins et al. (2018)

---

47 Corporate capture refers to the process by which corporations deliberately attempt to "dominate the information environment, so they can significantly affect decision-making" (Miller and Harkin 2010).

called into question the rationale for both the relatively weak regulatory approach taken toward alcohol and the continued participation of alcohol corporations in policy-making processes. The wedge between political decision-making and evidence-based scientific prevention policies and guidelines remains a challenge worldwide. Leaders and countries lack the political will or public health infrastructure to implement policies that have been found to be effective in reducing alcohol-related harm, including comprehensive alcohol marketing restrictions (Esser and Jernigan 2018). Commenting on restricting alcohol marketing, the WHO (2018) survey reveals (on the basis of advertising restrictiveness score) that many more persons are covered by policies that are the least restrictive or only slightly restrictive (28%) than are covered by policies that are very restrictive or the most restrictive (18%). Regarding the regulations governing the physical availability of alcohol, the WHO (2018) report adds that there was an overall trend of inadequate regulation, with 42 countries reporting no regulations on days or hours of sale since 2010. This calls for active campaigns by voluntary and community organizations to disseminate impartial scientific knowledge among voters. Collective efforts and societal commitment at the national level are needed to regulate the availability of alcohol to underage drinkers.

Hurdles in Enforcing the Legal Minimum Drinking Age Research and experience confirm that strong enforcement helps to reduce underage drinking by limiting access to alcohol, reducing opportunities for youth to drink, and curbing impaired driving. Despite the well-documented scientific evidence on the effectiveness of prevention policies for reducing alcohol misuse and related harm, the evidence from US studies suggests that effective alcohol control policies are not being widely implemented in US states (HHS, Office of the Surgeon General 2016). The study by Wolfson et al. (1995), related to the enforcement of minimum-age drinking laws in the US, reported various constraints on the enforcement of the minimum drinking age, which included the role of political factors (especially in sheriffs' departments), resource limitations, perceptions that punishments are inadequate, the time and effort required for processing and paperwork, and the poor record of enforcement of the minimum drinking age restrictions. Their findings also mentioned that officers reported facing a number of evidentiary and procedural challenges. Effective alcohol control policies are not being widely implemented in the US. The enforcement of underage drinking laws has often been found to be uneven, inconsistent, and sporadic, and outcomes generally diminish over time (Harding et al. 2016). The NHTSA (2001) has suggested that an aggressive law enforcement program, supported by strong laws and regulations, swift and sure consequences from the judiciary, and a strong prevention/education effort, would result in changed community social norms and changed behavior by youth.

Gaps Between Prevention Science and Practice Researchers have expressed concerns about the gap between science and practice in regard to the dissemination and implementation of more effective interventions. In the European region, which has the highest per capita alcohol consumption in the world, the member countries have not done enough to amend pricing policies in the line of WHO's "Best Buy" recommendations (WHO 2019). In addition, many countries in the region do not have a good record of reducing the negative consequences of drinking. In the Americas, alcohol marketing is widespread and pervasive in the form of electronic media advertisements, sponsorships of sporting teams and events, discount pricing, social media, and sales, etc. (PAHO 2015). Legal minimum age for buying and drinking alcohol is18 years in many European countries, which is less than legal minimum age of 21 in the US. Regarding the Americas, PAHO (2015) has observed that nearly 70% of the region's countries either lack regulations on advertising of alcoholic beverages, or their regulatory codes have been written by the alcohol industry itself. Further, evidence about this region also shows that only nine countries have alcohol taxes that reflect the amount of alcohol contained in beverages. Regarding the dangerous level of alcohol contents in the blood while driving, only five countries in the Americas (Brazil, Chile, Colombia, Ecuador, and Uruguay) have been found to have a statutory ceiling of less than 0.04 g/dl for blood alcohol concentration (PAHO 2015).

Wandersman et al. (2008) have suggested careful monitoring of three systems: the "Prevention Synthesis and Translation System" (distilling information about innovations and preparing them for implementation by end users), the "Prevention Support System" (conceptualized as supporting the work of those who will put the innovations into practice), and the "Prevention Delivery System" (implementation of innovations in the field). Spoth et al. (2009) have warned that there has been very limited research on interventions that target emerging alcohol use among late elementary school-aged children, high school students, and older adolescents not currently in college. In many countries, alcohol policies do not conform to the WHO's alcohol policy "best buys" recommendations, the aim of which is to limit physical availability by regulating the number and density of retail outlets that sell alcoholic beverages, the hours of the day or days of the week that beverages can be sold, and whether alcoholic beverages are to be sold for off-premises use only or for on-premises consumption (WHO 2004). In reviewing policy implementation across US states, SAMHSA (2016) noted that effective alcohol control policies were not being widely implemented despite well-documented, scientific evidence on the effectiveness of such policies for reducing alcohol misuse and related harm. This report also suggests the need to improve surveillance of risky drinking, drug use, and related problems.

Many countries are unable to implement the periodic and large-scale population surveys that are needed to collect information on underage drinking. Countries need to devote more resources to the regular collection of high-quality data, including those available in various governmental sectors that are not accessible nor analyzed (PAHO 2015). The WHO (2018) report recommends policies and interventions for monitoring and surveillance, including administering national surveys on alcohol consumption and related harm, designating entities to oversee data collection and dissemination, defining and tracking indicators of harmful alcohol use, maintaining data repositories, and developing evaluation mechanisms (WHO 2010).

4.2 Harm-Reduction Approach

GBD 2016 Alcohol Collaborators, in their study of alcohol use and burden for 195 countries over 1990-2016, came to the conclusion that "...the safest level of drinking is none" (P1026). These authors suggest that policies that focus on reducing population-level consumption will be most effective in reducing the health loss from alcohol use. Prevention programs, in essence are not meant to deal with situations of changing behavior in teens who are already engaged in harmful drinking (Leslie 2008). Harm-reduction interventions are needed to prevent problems by targeting risky contexts or patterns of use. Marlatt and Witkiewitz(2010) emphasize that "The primary goal of most harm-reduction approaches is to meet individuals "where they are at" and not to ignore or condemn the harmful behaviors but rather to work with the individual or community to minimize the harmful effects of a given behavior"(P591). Evidence suggests that rates of tobacco use, harmful alcohol use, and illicit drug use in young people can be reduced through the concerted application of a combination of regulatory, early-intervention, and harm-reduction approaches (Toumbourou et al. 2007).

Harm reduction is an umbrella term for interventions that aim to reduce the problematic effects of behaviors (Logan and Marlatt 2010). Several studies have demonstrated that controlled drinking is possible and that moderation-based treatments may be preferred over abstinence-only approaches (Marlatt and Witkiewitz 2002). Brief alcohol screening and intervention for college students (BASICS) is an example of a harm-reduction approach. This approach aims to motivate students to reduce risky behaviors, to promote healthier choices among young adults, and to provide important information and coping skills for risk reduction (Dimeff et al. 1999). Students can be identified through routine screening or through referrals from medical, housing, or disciplinary services.

Several empirical studies have demonstrated that harm-reduction approaches to alcohol problems are at least as effective as abstinence-oriented approaches at reducing alcohol consumption and alcohol-related consequences (Marlatt and Witkiewitz 2002). These interventions have been found to be effective in young people who are involved in risky alcohol use and injecting substance use (Toumbourou et al. 2007). Acknowledging that most adolescents and young adults will drink and supporting less harmful drinking behavior may be a means for providing education and prevention without provoking rebellious attitudes and behavior (Marlatt and Witkiewitz 2002). Harm reduction refers to policies and programs that aim to reduce the harm associated with the use of psychoactive substances. A defining feature of these policies is their focus on the prevention of drug-related harm rather than the prevention of drug use per se. The goals of therapy are the reduction of alcohol-related morbidity and mortality and the reduction of other social and economic problems related to chronic and excessive alcohol consumption (Marlatt and Witkiewitz 2002; Leslie et al. 2008). Harm-reduction strategies, including random breath testing and graduated driver licensing, have effectiveness evidence that they can reduce vehicle accidents and related death and injury (Toumbourou et al. 2007). Harm reduction is based on a philosophy of "starting where the user is at" and offers a pragmatic and compassionate approach to the prevention and treatment of the problem (Marlatt and Witkiewitz 2002; Jenkins et al. 2017).

4.3 Final Remarks on Prevention Policies

Underage drinking is a complex public health challenge because the developmental pathway from childhood to adulthood is marked by significant changes in risk for drinking and alcohol-related problems. Adolescence and young adulthood represent key periods during which substance use behavior can become established (Stockings et al. 2016). Evidence from multiple nationally representative surveys indicates that rates of alcohol use and binge alcohol use increase sharply between ages 12 and 21 (Masten et al. 2008).

Multiple risk factors likely interact, including the environment and possibly genetic factors, to increase the probability of alcohol problems developing in adolescence (Chartier et al. 2010). Due to the complicated interplay of biological maturation and environmental influence, public policy needs to develop strategies based on cross-disciplinary research involving developmental psychology, prevention, and neuroscience (Greenberg 2006; Steinberg 2011). Longitudinal and cross-disciplinary studies are critical to understanding the interrelationship between developmental stage and drinking behavior (Masten et al. 2008). Developmental/longitudinal evidence and the understanding of environmental influences can help public health authorities to design more effective population-based policies for preventing underage alcohol use

Working more broadly with families, schools, and communities, prevention scientists can find more effective ways to help people gain skills and formulate approaches to stop problem behaviors before they occur (NIDA 2003). More research is needed to assess the effectiveness of existing interventions about which little is known (SAMHSA 2016). This report has called for "enhanced public education to improve awareness about substance use problems." An authoritative parenting style and engagement with adolescents, community programs for adolescents to maintain healthy lifestyles, and the active involvement of schools in developing resilience skills and preventing antisocial activities (such as bullying) are deemed to be essential and critical links in supporting a healthy development pathway from childhood to adulthood. Recognizing the multi-domain nature of underage drinking and the harmful use of alcohol (binge drinking), concerted and integrated efforts are suggested to develop effective prevention, early interventions, and harm-reduction approaches.

SUMMARY

I n today's society, alcoholic beverages have been a routine part of the social landscape, as their use frequently accompanies socializing for many in the population (WHO 2018, Ch. 2). However, it is the harmful use of alcohol in the form of heavy episodic (binge) drinking, initiation of drinking in the underage population, comorbid use of alcohol with other substances (tobacco and drugs), alcohol dependence disorder, and use of alcohol in combination with mental disorders that become the source of an enormous disease burden (e.g., deaths, injuries, and disability) on society and require priority attention. Epidemiological evidence confirms that underage drinking increases steadily with age throughout the 12 to 20 range (National Research Council and Institute of Medicine 2003).

An expansive literature shows that alcohol intoxication can increase dysphoria, cognitive dysfunction, educational failure, impulsivity, and intensity of suicidal ideation, in addition to numerous other diseases (WHO 2018). This WHO report further adds that harm from drinking occurs not only to the drinker but also to those around him or her. The harm may take different forms, including road injuries from drunk driving, street violence and aggression, and damage to property. A national sampling of visits to hospital emergency departments in the US in 2011 (SAMHSA 2013) found a combination of alcohol and other drugs to be a major contributory factor to emergency cases.

Studies have shown that neuropsychiatric diseases (including AUDs) are among the most common disease categories that are entirely or partly caused by alcohol consumption (Rehm 2011). AUDs have risen from the eighth-largest contributor to death and disability globally in 1990 to the fifth largest in 2010 (WHO 2014a; Toumbourou et al. 2007). In addition to the strong empirical evidence of association between alcohol consumption and infectious diseases (such as HIV, tuberculosis, and respiratory infections), the relationship between alcohol consumption and major NCDs (such as cardiovascular disease, diabetes, cancer, liver diseases, and mental health disorders) is well documented in several research studies (WHO 2018). AUDs now rank first or second among mental and behavioral disorders in most of the developed countries and Eastern Europe. The results of country-level school surveys indicate that in many countries, alcohol use starts early in life—that is, before the age of 15 (WHO 2018). The prevalence of HED increases from the 15- to 19-age range to the 20-to-24 range (WHO 2018).

Data show considerable variations among regions and countries with respect to the prevalence of risky patterns of drinking among adolescents and youth. The prevalence rates of current drinking are highest among 15-19-year-olds in the WHO European region, followed by the region of the Americas and the Western Pacific region (WHO 2018). To account for regional variations in the prevalence of underage and binge drinking, an attempt is made to investigate the role of region-specific factors and economic affluence in explaining variations among regions. Focusing on the countries belonging to the regions of Europe and the Americas, two-way ANOVA[48] analysis is conducted. The data reveal that both factors—region-specific and economic development levels—explain the significant regional variations in the harmful use of alcohol by adolescents.

Underage drinking and its associated problems have profound negative consequences for underage drinkers themselves, their families, their communities, and society as a whole and contribute to a wide range of costly health and social problems (Harding et al. 2016). Alcohol use in adolescents is associated with neurocognitive alterations (in verbal learning, visual–spatial processing, memory and attention, and the development and integrity of the gray and white matter of the central nervous system) that seem to be related to behavioral, emotional, social, and academic problems in later life (WHO 2018). Age of initiation of alcohol use is important for at least two reasons. First, research in the US has found that the earlier people begin drinking, the more likely they are to become alcohol dependent in later life. Second, those who begin drinking in their teenage years are more likely to experience alcohol-related unintentional injuries (such as motor vehicle injuries, falls, burns, and drowning) than those who begin drinking at a later age (Jernigan 2001).

In addition to the problems related to early age of initiation, data from countries around the globe demonstrate a widespread culture of sporadic heavy, or binge, drinking among young people. Harmful patterns of drinking by adolescents interact with and are mediated by several environmental risk factors. Mediating risk factors include a permissive drinking culture in the society; weak enforcement of national laws in relation to minimum drinking age and access to harmful psychoactive substances; poor parenting style; inadequate skills-training programs in schools for resisting the influence of alcohol-using peers; weak administration in educational institutions to control unhealthy peer influence; and lack of community support networks. Excessive alcohol use is the single most important risk factor for injury and is by far the most promising yet underutilized

---

48 The two-way ANOVA compares the mean differences between groups that have been split on two independent variables (called factors).

target for injury-prevention programs (Gentilello et al. 2005). Evidence shows that in 2012, of the top five causes of YLDs in 15- to 19-year-old males worldwide, AUDs were ranked second (WHO 2012). The younger the individuals when they begin drinking alcohol, the greater the problems associated with alcohol misuse (Hawkins et al. 2007).

Because the harmful use of alcohol leads to a large burden of disease (communicable and non-communicable) and injury (intentional and unintentional) (WHO 2018), an attempt was made in this study to estimate the quantitative contributions of drinking patterns to AAFs, using WHO data for OECD countries. The OLS results highlight the significant role played by the prevalence of HED among adolescents and by the level of alcoholic spirits consumed in explaining the AAFs. These results are corroborated by other studies in this field. Existing research studies have shown that alcohol consumption has been responsible for a large proportion of the total mortality burden among people of younger ages (Shield and Rehm 2015; see also citations in WHO 2018, p. 78, for other studies). The quantitative effects of drinking patterns on the alcohol-attributable burden of disease have also been demonstrated in several economic studies (WHO 2018). The study also made an attempt to determine what drinking pattern and type of drink can be considered harmful. Using the pattern of drinking score (PDS)[49] data from the WHO (2018), the ordinal regression technique was used to understand the factors of risky patterns of drinking among countries. It was found that the probability of increasing PDS increases with an increase in episodic drinking and the volume of spirits consumed by the underage population.

The multiple individual and environmental risk factors mentioned above warrant cognizance when designing prevention and intervention programs. Evidence-based macro-level prevention strategies for excessive drinking (e.g., increasing alcohol taxes, regulating alcohol-outlet density, and having commercial-host liability laws)[50] could help reduce underage drinking and related harm (Esser et al. 2017). In addition to the macro-level factors, there are various proximate contextual factors, such as association with friends and the role of parental and neighborhood factors that affect adolescents' development trajectory and health behavior. Peer networks are a salient reference group for youth, with peers playing a particularly important and influential role in helping shape adolescents' evolving social worlds (Wang et al. 2015). Parents also play an equally influential role in adolescents' social worlds, affecting both adolescents' friendship-tie choices and drinking behavior. Early initiation to alcohol use and its progression highly increase the odds of

---

49   PDS data is available from the WHO on a scale from 1 (least risky pattern of drinking) to 5 (most risky pattern of drinking).

50   Normally, laws impose criminal or other liability on individuals who allow underage drinking events on property they own, lease, or otherwise control. Social-host liability refers to laws that impose civil liability on non- commercial alcohol providers for harms caused by their intoxicated or underage drinking guests (Harding et al. 2016).

discontinuing school education and adopting drugs. Universal prevention efforts ought to target adolescents generally, and more special efforts should focus on those who are at risk of dropping out of high school. The failure to complete high school has intergenerational implications for socioeconomic attainment because children whose parents did not complete high school are more likely to perform poorly in school, with the eventual risk of dropping out themselves (Tice 2013).

There is, thus, an urgent need for early interventions in multiple domains. Because there are both risk and protective factors within and across family, peer, school, and community environments, studies have emphasized the need for interventions that involve several social domains (Catalano et al. 2004). On the basis of a meta-analytical review of 177 primary prevention programs, Durlak and Wells (1997) suggested that interventions that both decrease problems and increase competencies might ultimately be more effective in lessening the probability of future dysfunction than programs that only reduce problems or symptoms.

The following is a list of broad recommendations based on some prominent research studies on preventing adolescent risks of substance use. It is important to point out that studies emphasize that multicomponent programs (combining multiple approaches, such as family, school programs, country's laws and norms, early childhood development programs, etc.) tend to be more effective than a single program alone:

- Promoting health development through universal childhood development interventions, including the prenatal period through age eight (NIDA 2016)
- Arranging programs of prenatal and early-childhood home visitation by nurses in high-risk families (Olds et al. 1998)
- Educating parents about proactive and authoritative parenting styles (Hawkins et al. 1992; Borawski et al. 2003) through community and public workshops
- Educating parents about the early warning signs related to the risks of substance use by teenagers (Ali et al. 2011)
- Preventing early initiation of substance use (Petraitis, Flay, and Miller 1995; Hawkins, Catalano, and Miller 1992) through controlling risk factors and developing protective factors
- Implementing preventive screening programs in schools that first identify risk factors or early phenotypic features (e.g., behaviors and biomarkers), whose presence in individuals makes the development of psychological or behavioral problems more likely (O'Connell et al. 2009)
- Introducing school-based skills-training curricula to increase resilience and resist peer pressure to engage in substance use (Stigler et al. 2011; Hodder et al. 2011; Komro et al. 2002)

- Adopting policies to increase educational attainment and the prevention of school dropouts (Christenson and Thurlow 2004)
- Strictly enforcing the WHO's "best buy" recommendations (WHO 2018; Komro et al. 2002)
- Organizing community-based social networks associating adolescents in pro-social activities, teamwork, and sports, as well as emotional learning, vocational training, and volunteering programs (Hansen, Larson, and Dworkin 2003)
- Designing community projects geared toward changing attitudes and beliefs about drinking (Cook and Moore 2002)
- Conducting public education and campaign programs on maintaining a healthy lifestyle (Bandura 2004)
- Monitoring trends (through regular surveillance efforts) in underage alcohol consumption and alcohol-related morbidity and mortality (Chen et al. 2013)
- Early-intervention and harm-reduction approaches (with moderation goals) (Stockings et al. 2016; Marlatt and Witkiewitz 2002; Toumbourou et al. 2007)

Globally, efforts to promote alcohol use have increased in both prevalence and sophistication in the past 30 years. Prevention technologies, however, have not kept pace with the spread of new and potentially harmful patterns of drinking nor with the expansion of promotional activities, despite the fact that there are numerous strategies that have been found to be effective, at least in developed nations (Jernigan 2001). In reality, the gap between scientific prevention policies and government policies is growing. Many developed countries are relaxing controls on availability, sale, and pricing. Alcoholic-beverage marketers have intensified their targeting of young drinkers in recent years, introducing an array of inexpensive new products, such as alcopops, alcoholic "energy" drinks, and premixed cocktails, with recipes and packaging designed to appeal to young people (Jernigan 2001). The global alcohol market is dominated by a few multinationals whose concentrated resources fuel the worldwide expansion of alcohol marketing. Building a web of subsidiaries and joint ventures, these companies are using marketing technologies that have been tested and, in some cases, banned in developed countries to promote alcohol consumption in the developing world (Jernigan 1997).

Essentially, the persistence and high prevalence of underage drinking remain a considerable public health challenge despite the advances in preventive science and their applications in the last few years. While many high-income countries participate in school surveys, data on alcohol consumption among young people from low-income countries are scarce. It is hoped that through active collaboration between neuroscientists and scholars from health, social science, and epidemiological disciplines, effective prevention and intervention programs can be designed to check the menace of drinking and drug abuse among adolescents and young adults. Finally, but not of least importance, the success of evidence-based public policies ultimately depends upon the resources made available by politicians and their commitments to implement the policies. However, the policies that are followed in practice are governed by the myopic "revenue greed" of the "power elite," even though these policies often ultimately run against mass social well-being. The real solution to underage drinking will remain elusive unless the ruling elite surrender their narrow interests and follow evidence-based scientific policies that protect youth against multiple risk factors. Harm-reduction approaches (including the rehabilitation of substance users) are suggested to complement the prevention-alone (zero-tolerance) interventions with the aim of reducing the high burden of substance use among adolescents and youth. The integration of the ongoing advances in neurosciences with an increased understanding of the complex interplay between biological and behavioral changes from early childhood to adolescence is expected to help public health authorities to design more effective evidence-supported policies.

REFERENCES

Adler, N.E. and Newman, K. (2002). Socioeconomic disparities in health: Pathways and policies. *Health Affairs, 34(1)*, 6–14.

Agerwala, S., and McCance-Katz, E. (2012). Integrating screening, brief intervention, and referral to treatment (SBIRT) into clinical practice settings: A brief review. *Journal of Psychoactive Drugs, 44*(4), 301–317.

Agresti Alan (2018): Statistical Methods for Social Sciences, Fifth Edition Pearson Education

Ahlström SK, Österberg EL. International Perspectives on Adolescent and Young Adult Drinking. *Alcohol Res Health.* 2004;28(4):258–268. *PubMed Central PMCID: PMC6601676.*

Anderson, P., Jané-Llopis, E., and Hosman, C. (2011). Reducing the silent burden of impaired mental health. *Health Promotion International, 26* (suppl 1), i4–19. doi:10.1093/heapro/dar051

Babor TF, Robaina K, Noel JK, Ritson EB(2017). Vulnerability to alcohol-related problems: a policy brief with implications for the regulation of alcohol marketing. *Addiction. 2017;112(S1):94–101*

Babor, T., McRee, B., Kassebaum, P., Grimaldi, P., Ahmed, K., and Bray, J. (2007). Screening, brief intervention, and referral to treatment (SBIRT) toward a public health approach to the management of substance abuse. *Substance Abuse, 28*, 7–30.

Beccaria F. and White H.R. (2012): Underage Drinking in Europe and North America, Ch 1 in Philippe De White and Mack C. Mitchell Jr. Edited Underage Drinking. *A Report on Drinking in the Second Decade of Life in Europe and North America.*

Benegal, V., Chand, P., and Obot, I. (2009). Packages of care for alcohol use disorders in low- and middle-income countries. *PloS Med, 6*(10): e1000170.

Benoit K(2011); Linear Regression Models with Logarithmic Transformations, *London School of Economics, London, Vol 22, Issue 1*, Pages 22-36

Black, M. M., Walker, S. P., Fernald, L., Andersen, C. T., DiGirolamo, A. M., Lu, C., McCoy, D. C., Fink, G., Shawar, Y. R., Shiffman, J., Devercelli, A. E., Wodon, Q. T., Vargas-Barón, E., Grantham-McGregor, S., & Lancet Early Childhood Development Series Steering Committee (2017). Early childhood development coming of age: science through the life course. *Lancet (London, England), 389(10064), 77–90.* https://doi.org/10.1016/S0140-6736(16)31389-7

Botelho, R., and Richmond, R. (1996). Secondary prevention of excessive alcohol use: Assessing the prospects of implementation. *Family Practice, 13,* 182–193

Bouchery, E., Harwood, H., Sacks, J., Simon, C., and Brewer, R. (2011). Economic costs of excessive alcohol consumption in the US, 2006. *American Journal of Preventive Medicine, 41*(5), 516 524.

Bräker A. B., Soellner R. Alcohol drinking cultures of European adolescents. *Eur J Public Health 2016;* 26: 581–586.

Bränström R, Sjöström E, and Andréasson S(2008): Individual, group and community risk and protective factors for alcohol and drug use among Swedish adolescents, *European Journal of Public Health*, Volume 18, Issue 1, February 2008, Pages 12–18

Britto, P. R., Lye, S. J., Proulx, K., Yousafzai, A. K., Matthews, S. G., Vaivada, T., Perez-Escamilla, R., Rao, N., Ip, P., Fernald, L. C. H., MacMillan, H., Hanson, M., Wachs, T. D., Yao, H., Yoshikawa, H., Cerezo, A., Leckman, J. F., Bhutta, Z. A., & Early Childhood Development Interventions Review Group, Lancet Early Childhood Development Series Steering Committee. (2017). Advancing Early Childhood Development: From Science to Scale 2: Nurturing care: Promoting early childhood development. *The Lancet,* 389(10064), 91–102.

Bröning, S., Kumpfer, K., Kruse, K., Sack, P. M., Schaunig-Busch, I., Ruths, S., … Thomasius, R. (2012). Selective prevention programs for children from substance-affected families: a comprehensive systematic review. *Substance abuse treatment, prevention, and policy, 7,* 23. doi:10.1186/1747-597X-7-23

Brown SA, McGue M, Maggs J, Schulenberg J, Hingson R, Swartzwelder S, Martin C, Chung T, Tapert SF, Sher K, Winters KC, Lowman C, Murphy S. A(2008): Developmental perspective on alcohol and youths 16 to 20 years of age. *Pediatrics. 2008* Apr;121 Suppl 4(Suppl 4):S290-310. doi: 10.1542/peds.2007-2243D. PMID: 18381495; PMCID: PMC2765460.

Cash, S., and Bridge, J. (2009). Epidemiology of youth suicide and suicidal behavior. *Current Opinion in Pediatrics, 21*(5), 613–619.

Casswell S(2013). Vested interests in addiction research and policy. Why do we not see the corporate interests of the alcohol industry as clearly as we see those of the tobacco industry? *Addiction* 2013;108:680–5

Catalano, R F(2018): The Surgeon General's Report on Alcohol, Drugs, and Health: A Focus on Prevention Facing Addiction in America, *Prevention Section Editor*

Catalano, R. F., Fagan, A. A., Gavin, L. E., Greenberg, M. T., Irwin, C. E., Jr, Ross, D. A., & Shek, D. T. (2012). Worldwide application of prevention science in adolescent health. *Lancet (London, England), 379*(9826), 1653–1664. doi:10.1016/S0140-6736(12)60238-4

Catalano, R., and Hawkins, J. (1996). The social development model: A theory of antisocial behaviour. In J. Hawkins (Ed.), *Delinquency and crime* (pp. 149–197). New York: Cambridge University Press.

Catalano, R., Berglund, M., Ryan, J., Lonczak, H., and Hawkins, J. (2004). Positive youth development in the United States: Research findings on evaluations of positive youth development programs. *Annals of the American Academy of Political and Social Science, 591*(1), 98–124.

Catalano, R., Haggerty, K., Osterele, S., Fleming, C., and Hawkins, J. (2004). The importance of bonding to school for healthy development: Findings from the social development research group. *Journal of School Health, 74*, 252–261.

Charlois T(2010): Early intervention targeting youth at risk and European cities, document ref. no. P-PG/COOP (2010) 12, *7th EXASS Net meeting in Oslo, Norway 2 - 4 June 2010, European network of partnerships between stakeholders at frontline level responding to drug problems providing experience and assistance for inter-sectoral cooperation,* https://rm.coe.int/7th-exass-net-meeting-in-oslo-norway-2-4-june-2010-early-intervention-/168075f9a5

Chartier, K. G., Hesselbrock, M. N., & Hesselbrock, V. M. (2010). Development and vulnerability factors in adolescent alcohol use. *Child and adolescent psychiatric clinics of North America,* 19(3), 493–504. doi:10.1016/j.chc.2010.03.004

Cheng ATA, Gau S, Chen THH, Chang J, Chang Y(2004). A 4-Year Longitudinal Study on Risk Factors for Alcoholism. *Arch Gen Psychiatry.* 2004;61(2):184–191.

Cherpitel C. J. (2013). Focus on: the burden of alcohol use—trauma and emergency outcomes. *Alcohol research : current reviews, 35*(2), 150–154.

Chisholm D., Moro D., Bertram M., Pretorius C., Gmel G., Shield K.D., Rehm J(2018). Are the "best buys" for alcohol control still valid? An update on the comparative cost-effectiveness of alcohol control strategies at the global level. *J. Stud. Alcohol Drugs.* 2018;79:514–522

Conrod P.J., Castellanos N., Mackie C.(2008): Personality-targeted interventions delay the growth of adolescent drinking and binge drinking. *J. Child Psychol. Psychiatry.* 2008;49:181–190

Conrod P.J., O'Leary-Barrett M., Newton N., Topper L., Castellanos-Ryan N., Mackie C., Girard A(2013). Effectiveness of a selective, personality-targeted prevention program for adolescent alcohol use and misuse: A cluster randomized controlled trial. *JAMA Psychiatry.* 2013;70:334–342

Cook, W. K., Bond, J., & Greenfield, T. K. (2014). Are alcohol policies associated with alcohol consumption in low- and middle-income countries?. *Addiction (Abingdon, England), 109*(7), 1081–1090. https://doi.org/10.1111/add.12571

Cooper ML, Frone MR, Russell M, Mudar P.(1995) Drinking to regulate positive and negative emotions: a motivational model of alcohol use. *J Pers Soc Psychol* (1995) 69(5):990–1005. 10.1037//0022-3514.69.5.990

Costello, E. J., and Angold, A. (1995). Developmental epidemiology. In D. Cicchetti and D. J. Cohen (Eds.), *Wiley series on personality processes. Developmental psychopathology, Vol. 1. Theory and methods* (pp. 23–56). Oxford, England: John Wiley and Sons.

Courtney, K. E., & Polich, J. (2009). Binge drinking in young adults: Data, definitions, and determinants. *Psychological bulletin*, 135(1), 142–156. doi:10.1037/a0014414

Crews, F. T., Vetreno, R. P., Broadwater, M. A., & Robinson, D. L. (2016). Adolescent Alcohol Exposure Persistently Impacts Adult Neurobiology and Behavior. *Pharmacological reviews*, 68(4), 1074–1109. doi:10.1124/pr.115.012138

De Bellis MD, Narasimhan A, Thatcher DL, Keshavan MS, Soloff P, Clark DB(2005). Prefrontal cortex, thalamus, and cerebellar volumes in adolescents and young adults with adolescent-onset alcohol use disorders and comorbid mental disorders. *Alcohol Clin Exp Res* (2005) 29(9):1590–600.

Dimeff, Linda A, Baer, John S, Kivlahan, Daniel R, Marlatt, G Alan(1999): Brief Alcohol Screening and Intervention for College Students (Basics): A Harm Reduction Approach *Paperback, Guilford Publications*

Donovan, J. E., & Molina, B. S. (2011). Childhood risk factors for early-onset drinking. *Journal of studies on alcohol and drugs*, 72(5), 741–751. doi:10.15288/jsad.2011.72.741

Durlak, J., and Wells, A. (1997). Primary prevention mental health programs for children and adolescents: A meta-analytic review. *American Journal of Community Psychology, 25(2), 115–52.*

Elder, R., Lawrence, B., Ferguson, A., Naimi, T., Brewer, R., Chattopadhyah, S., … Fielding, J. (2010). Task force on community preventive services: The effectiveness of tax policy interventions for reducing excessive alcohol consumption and related harms. *American Journal of Preventive Medicine, 38(2), 217–29.*

Esser MB and Jernigan DH(2018): Policy Approaches for Regulating Alcohol Marketing in a Global Context: A Public Health Perspective. *Annu Rev Public Health.* 2018 Apr 1;39:385-401

Fagan, A. A., Hawkins, J. D., & Catalano, R. F. (2011). Engaging communities to prevent underage drinking. Alcohol research & health : *The journal of the National Institute on Alcohol Abuse and Alcoholism,* 34(2), 167–174.

Fillmore, M. T., & Jude, R. (2011). Defining "binge" drinking as five drinks per occasion or drinking to a .08% BAC: which is more sensitive to risk?. *The American journal on addictions,* 20(5), 468–475

Foster SE, Vaughan RD, Foster WH, Califano JA. Alcohol consumption and expenditures for underage drinking and adult excessive drinking. *JAMA.* 2003;289(8):989–995

Foxcroft DR, Tsertsvadze A(2011). Universal school-based prevention programs for alcohol misuse in young people. *Cochr Database Syst Rev.* CD009113. 10.1002/14651858. CD009113

Friese B and Grube J W (2001): Youth Drinking Rates and Problems: A Comparison of European Countries and the United States, Prevention Research Center Pacific *Institute for Research and Evaluation* http://www.udetc.org/documents/YouthDrinkingRatesandProblems.pdf

Gallimberti L, Chindamo S, Buja A, Forza G, Tognazzo F, Galasso L, Vinelli A, Baldo V. Underage drinking on saturday nights, sociodemographic and environmental risk factors: a cross-sectional study. *Subst Abuse Treat Prev Policy.* 2011 Jul 5;6:15. doi: 10.1186/1747-597X-6-15. PMID: 21729273; PMCID: PMC3152933.

Gary Roberts and Associates (2008): Best Practices for Preventing Substance Use Problem in Nova Scotia. November 2008. *Nova Scotia Health Promotion and Protection Services. Halifax, NS*

GBD 2016 Alcohol and Drug Use Collaborators. The global burden of disease attributable to alcohol and drug use in 195 countries and territories, 1990–2016: a systematic analysis for the Global Burden of Disease Study 2016. *The Lancet Psychiatry.* 1 Nov 2018.

Ghasemi, A., and Zahediasl, S. (2012). Normality tests for statistical analysis: A guide for non-statisticians. *International Journal of Endocrinology and Metabolism, 10*(2), 486–489.

Gonzales, K. R., Largo, T. W., Miller, C., Kanny, D., & Brewer, R. D. (2015). Consumption of Alcoholic Beverages and Liquor Consumption by Michigan High School OECD (2020), *Alcohol consumption (indicator).* doi: 10.1787/e6895909-en (Accessed on 15 March 2020

Gordon, R. (1983). An operational classification of disease prevention. *Public Health Reports, 98*, 107–109.

Grant, B., and Dawson, D. (1997). Age at onset of alcohol use and its association with DSM-IV alcohol abuse and dependence: Results from the national longitudinal alcohol epidemiologic survey. *Journal of Substance Abuse, 9*, 103–110.

Greenberg M. T. (2006). Promoting resilience in children and youth. *Ann. N.Y. Acad. Sci. 1094, 139–150. 10.1196/annals.1376.013*

Griffin, K., and Botvin, G. (2011). Evidence-based interventions for preventing substance use disorders in adolescents. *Child and Adolescent Psychiatric Clinics of North America Journal, 19*(3), 505–526.

Griffiths, W. E. & Hill, R. Carter. & Lim, G. C. (2012): Principles of econometrics. *Danvers, MA: John Wiley & Sons*

Gruenewald P. J. (2011). Regulating availability: how access to alcohol affects drinking and problems in youth and adults. *Alcohol research & health: The journal of the National Institute on Alcohol Abuse and Alcoholism*, 34(2), 248–256.

Guttmannova, K., Bailey, J. A., Hill, K. G., Lee, J. O., Hawkins, J. D., Woods, M. L., & Catalano, R. F. (2011). Sensitive periods for adolescent alcohol use initiation: predicting the lifetime occurrence and chronicity of alcohol problems in adulthood. *Journal of studies on alcohol and drugs*, 72(2), 221–231. doi:10.15288/jsad.2011.72.221

Hahn RA, Kuzara JL, Elder R, Brewer R, Chattopadhyay S, Fielding J, et al. (2010) Effectiveness of policies restricting hours of alcohol sales in preventing excessive alcohol consumption and related harms. *Am J Prev Med* 39: 590–604. 10.1016/j. amepre.2010.09.016

Harding, Frances M.,Hingson, Ralph W.,Klitzner, Michael, Mosher, James F.,Brown, Jorielle, Vincent, Robert M.,Dahl, Elizabeth, Cannon, Carol L.(2016): Underage Drinking. A Review of Trends and Prevention Strategies, *Am J Prev Med* 2016;51(4S2):S148–S157)

Hawkins JD, Graham JW, Maguin E, Abbott R, Hill KG, Catalano RF(1997). Exploring the effects of age of alcohol use initiation and psychosocial risk factors on subsequent alcohol misuse. *J Stud Alcohol.* 1997 May;58(3):280-90. doi: 10.15288/jsa.1997.58.280. PMID: 9130220; PMCID: PMC1894758.

Hawkins, B., Holden, C., Eckhardt, J., & Lee, K. (2018). Reassessing policy paradigms: A comparison of the global tobacco and alcohol industries. *Global public health*, 13(1), 1–19. doi:10.1080/17441692.2016.1161815

Hawkins, J., and Weis, J. (1985). The social development model: An integrated approach to delinquency prevention. *Journal of Primary Prevention, 6*(2), 73–97.

Hawkins, J., Catalano, R., and Arthur, M. (2002, Nov-Dec). Promoting science-based prevention in communities. *Addictive Behaviors, 27*(6), 951–76.

Hawkins, J., Catalano, R., and Miller, J. (1992). Risk and protective factors for alcohol and other drug problems in adolescence and early adulthood: Implications for substance abuse prevention. *Psychological Bulletin, 112*(1), 64–105.

Healey, C., Rahman, A., Faizal, M.A., & Kinderman, P. (2014). Underage drinking in the UK: changing trends, impact and interventions. A rapid evidence synthesis. The International journal on drug policy, 25 1, 124-32.

Holder D (2000): Community prevention of alcohol problems, Session: School and Community Interventions: *Richard Clayton, Chair, Addictive Behaviors*, Vol. 25, No. 6, pp. 843–859, 2000

IARD (2019: Trends Report Heavy Episodic Drinking, *The International Alliance for Responsible Drinking (IARD)*, October 2019

Jané-Llopis, E., Anderson, P., Stewart-Brown, S., Weare, K., Wahlbeck, K., McDaid, D., . . . Litchfield, P. (2011). Reducing the silent burden of impaired mental health. *Journal of Health Communication, 16* (Suppl 2), 59–74.

Jenkins, E. K., Slemon, A., & Haines-Saah, R. J. (2017). Developing harm reduction in the context of youth substance use: insights from a multi-site qualitative analysis of young people's harm minimization strategies. *Harm reduction journal,* 14(1), 53. doi:10.1186/s12954-017-0180-z

Johnson CA, Pentz MA, Weber MD, Dwyer JH, Baer N, Mackinnon DP, et al(1990). Relative effectiveness of comprehensive community programming for drug abuse prevention with high-risk and low-risk adolescents. *Journal of Consulting & Clinical Psychology* 1990;58(4):447-56.

Johnston, L. D., Miech, R. A., O'Malley, P. M., Bachman, J. G., Schulenberg, J. E., & Patrick, M. E. (2018). Monitoring the Future national survey results on drug use: 1975-2017: Overview, key findings on adolescent drug use. *Ann Arbor: Institute for Social Research, The University of Michigan.*

Jones, L., Bellis, M.A., Dedman, D., Sumnall, H., Tocque, K (2008). Alcohol-attributable fractions for England: Alcohol-attributable mortality and hospital admissions.

Juergens J and Hampton D(2019): Widespread Underage Drinking, Addiction Centre USA

Kaplow, J. B., Curran, P. J., Dodge, K. A., & Conduct Problems Prevention Research Group (2002). Child, parent, and peer predictors of early-onset substance use: a multisite longitudinal study. *Journal of abnormal child psychology*, 30(3), 199–216. doi:10.1023/a:1015183927979

Kelly-Weeder, S., Phillips, K., and Rounseville, S. (2011). Effectiveness of public health programs for decreasing alcohol consumption. *PI Patient Intelligence, (3), 29–29.*

Kieling C, Baker-Henningham H, Belfer M, Conti G, Ertem I, Omigbodun O, et al. Child and adolescent mental health worldwide: evidence for action. *Lancet.* 2011;378:1515–1525. 10.1016/S0140-6736(11)60827-1

Kohn, R., Saxena, S., Levav, I., and Saraceno, B. (2004). The treatment gap in mental healthcare. *Bulletin of the World Health Organization, 82*(11), 858–866.

Komro, K., and Toomey, T. (2002). Strategies to prevent underage drinking. *Alcohol Research and Health, 26*, 5–14.

Korotayev A, Khaltourina D, Meshcherina K, and Zamiatnina E(2018), Distilled Spirits Overconsumption as the Most Important Factor of Excessive Adult Male Mortality in Europe, *Alcohol and Alcoholism*, Volume 53, Issue 6, November 2018, Pages 742–752,

Kuklinski, M. R., Fagan, A. A., Hawkins, J. D., Briney, J. S., & Catalano, R. F. (2015). Benefit-Cost Analysis of a Randomized Evaluation of Communities That Care: Monetizing Intervention Effects on the Initiation of Delinquency and Substance Use Through Grade 12. *Journal of experimental criminology*, 11(2), 165–192. doi:10.1007/s11292-014-9226-3

Lachenmeier, D. W., Monakhova, Y. B., & Rehm, J. (2014). Influence of unrecorded alcohol consumption on liver cirrhosis mortality. *World journal of gastroenterology*, 20(23), 7217–7222. https://doi.org/10.3748/wjg.v20.i23.7217

Lammers J, Goossens F, Conrod P, Engels R, Wiers RW, Kleinjan M. Effectiveness of a selective intervention program targeting personality risk factors for alcohol misuse among young adolescents: results of a cluster randomized controlled trial. *Addiction* (2015) 110:1101–9. doi: 10.1111/add.12952

Lancet Public Health (2018): Addressing youth drinking, Editorial, Vol 3 February 2018 e52

Leslie KM. Harm reduction(2008): An approach to reducing risky health behaviors in adolescents. *Paediatr Child Health*. 2008;13(1):53–60. PubMed.

Leyton, M., and Stewart, S. (Eds.). (2014). Substance abuse in Canada: Childhood and adolescent pathways to substance use disorders. Ottawa, ON: *Canadian Centre on Substance Abuse.*

Lipari R N, Van Horn S L, Hughes A, and, Williams M(2017): Underage Binge Drinking Varies Within and Across States, *SAMHSA The CBSHQ Report*

Liu, Xing (2009) "Ordinal Regression Analysis: Fitting the Proportional Odds Model Using Stata, SAS and SPSS," *Journal of Modern Applied Statistical Methods*: Vol. 8 : Iss. 2, Article 30.

LoConte NK, Brewster AM, Kaur JS, Merrill JK, Alberg AJ. Alcohol and cancer: a statement of the American Society of Clinical Oncology. *J Clin Oncol.* 2018;36:83-93. doi:10.1200/JCO.2017.76.1155

Logan, D. E., & Marlatt, G. A. (2010). Harm reduction therapy: a practice-friendly review of research. *Journal of clinical psychology*, 66(2), 201–214. doi:10.1002/jclp.20669

Lopez-Quintero, C., Hasin, D. S., de Los Cobos, J. P., Pines, A., Wang, S., Grant, B. F., & Blanco, C. (2011). Probability and predictors of remission from life-time nicotine, alcohol, cannabis or cocaine dependence: results from the National Epidemiologic Survey on Alcohol and Related Conditions. *Addiction (Abingdon, England)*, 106(3), 657–669. doi:10.1111/j.1360-0443.2010.03194.x

Lubman, D., and Yücel, M. (2008). Editorial: Drugs, mental health and the adolescent brain: Implications for early intervention. *Early Intervention in Psychiatry, 2*, 63–66.

MacArthur, G. J., Smith, M. C., Melotti, R., Heron, J., Macleod, J., Hickman, M., Kipping, R. R., Campbell, R., & Lewis, G. (2012). Patterns of alcohol use and multiple risk behaviour by gender during early and late adolescence: the ALSPAC cohort. *Journal of public health (Oxford, England), 34 Suppl 1*(Suppl 1), i20–i30.

Madras, B., Compton, W., Avula, D., Stegbauer, T., Stein, J., and Clark, H. (2009). Screening, brief interventions, referral to treatment (SBIRT) for illicit drug and alcohol use at multiple healthcare sites: Comparison at intake and six months. *Drug and Alcohol Dependence, 99*(1–3), 280–295.

Maggs, J., and Schuleberg, J. (2004/2005). Trajectories of alcohol use during the transition to adulthood. *Alcohol Research and Health, 28*, 195–201.

Manhica, H., Lundin, A., & Danielsson, A. K. (2019). Not in education, employment, or training (NEET) and risk of alcohol use disorder: a nationwide register-linkage study with 485

Manthey, J., Imtiaz, S., Neufeld, M., Rylett, M., & Rehm, J. (2017). Quantifying the global contribution of alcohol consumption to cardiomyopathy. *Population health metrics*, *15*(1), 20. https://doi.org/10.1186/s12963-017-0137-1

Manthey, J., Shield, K., Rylett, M., Hasan, O.S.M, Probst, C., & Rehm, J. (2019). Alcohol exposure between 1990 and 2017 and forecasts until 2030: a global modelling study. *Lancet*. doi: 10.1016/S0140-6736(18)32744-

Marlatt G A and Witkiewitz K(2010): Update on Harm-Reduction Policy and Intervention Research, Annu. Rev. Clin. *Psychol*. 2010. 6:591–606

Marlatt G. A., Witkiewitz K.(2002): Harm reduction approaches to alcohol use: Health promotion, prevention, and treatment. *Addict. Behav.* 27, 867–886 (2002)

Marlatt, G., and Witkiewitz, K. (2002). Harm reduction approaches to alcohol use: Health promotion prevention and treatment. *Addictive Behaviors, 27*, 867–886.

Marshall, E J (2014): Adolescent Alcohol Use: Risks and Consequences, *Alcohol and Alcoholism*, Volume 49, Issue 2, March/April 2014, Pages 160–164.

Martin J., Barry J., Goggin D., Morgan K., Ward M., and O'Suilleabhain T., "Alcohol-attributable mortality in Ireland." *Alcohol2010*. Jul-Aug;45(4):379–386.

Masten, A. S., Faden, V. B., Zucker, R. A., & Spear, L. P. (2009). A developmental perspective on underage alcohol use. *Alcohol research & health : the journal of the National Institute on Alcohol Abuse and Alcoholism*, 32(1), 3–15.

Masten, A., and Coatsworth, J. (1998). The development of competence in favorable and unfavorable environments: Lessons from research on successful children. *American Psychologist, 53*(2), 205–220.

McCambridge, J., Hawkins, B., & Holden, C. (2014). Vested interests in addiction research and policy. The challenge corporate lobbying poses to reducing society's alcohol problems: insights from UK evidence on minimum unit pricing. *Addiction (Abingdon, England)*, 109(2), 199–205. doi:10.1111/add.12380

McCarty C., Ebel B., Garrison M., DiGiuseppe D., Christakis D., Rivara F. Continuity of binge and harmful drinking from late adolescence to early adulthood. *Pediatrics.* 2004;114(3):714;

McClellan, A., and Meyers, K. (2004). Contemporary addiction treatment: A review of the literature. *Biology and Psychiatry, 56,* 764–770.

Medina-Mora ME. Prevention of substance abuse (2005): a brief overview. *World Psychiatry.* 2005 Feb;4(1):25–30. PubMed PMID: 16633497; PubMed Central PMCID: PMC1414714.

Merikangas, K. R., and McClair, V. L. (2012). Epidemiology of substance use disorders. *Human genetics, 131*(6), 779–89.

Merline, A., Jager, J., & Schulenberg, J. E. (2008). Adolescent risk factors for adult alcohol use and abuse: stability and change of predictive value across early and middle adulthood. *Addiction (Abingdon, England),* 103 Suppl 1(Suppl 1), 84–99. doi:10.1111/j.1360-0443.2008.02178.x

Miller D and Harkins C (2010) Corporate strategy, corporate capture: food and alcohol industry lobbying and public health. Crit Soc Policy 30: 564–589.

Miller J.W., Naimi T.S., Brewer R.D., and Jones S.E (2007), "Binge drinking and associated health risk behaviors among high school students." Pediatrics.;119(1):76–85. doi: 10.1542/peds.2006-1517

Mitchell, S., Gryczynski, J., O'Grady, K., and Schwartz, R. (2013). SBIRT for adolescent drug and alcohol use: Current status and future directions. *Journal of Substance Abuse, 44*(5), 463–472.

Monico N(2019): Binge Drinking Statistics, Alcohol.ORG ; Viner RM, Taylor B. Adult outcomes of binge drinking in adolescence: findings from a UK national birth cohort. *J Epidemiol Community Health.* 2007 Oct;61(10):902-7. doi: 10.1136/ jech.2005.038117. PMID: 17873228; PMCID: PMC2652971.;

Monteriro M G (2016): Public policies to prevent alcohol-related harm, Epidemiol. Serv. Saúde vol.25 no.*1 Brasília Jan./Mar.* 2016

Moodie R., Stuckler D., Monteiro C., Sheron N., Neal B., Thamarangsi T., Lincoln P., Casswell S.(2013): Profits and pandemics: Prevention of harmful effects of tobacco, alcohol, and ultra-processed food and drink industries. *Lancet.* 2013;381:670–679.

Moore GF, Rothwell H, Segrott J. An exploratory study of the relationship between parental attitudes and behaviour and young people's consumption of alcohol. *Subst Abuse Treat Prev Policy.* 2010 Apr 22; 5:6. doi: 10.1186/1747–597X-5–6. PubMed PMID: 20412576; PubMed Central PMCID: PMC2865449

Mukamal KJ, Kuller LH, Fitzpatrick AL, Longstreth WT Jr, Mittleman MA, Siscovick DS(2003). Prospective study of alcohol consumption and risk of dementia in older adults. *JAMA.* 2003;289(11):1405-1413. doi:10.1001/jama.289.11.1405

Nagel, B. J., Schweinsburg, A. D., Phan, V., & Tapert, S. F. (2005). Reduced hippocampal volume among adolescents with alcohol use disorders without psychiatric comorbidity. *Psychiatry research*, 139(3), 181–190

Naimi, T. S., Siegel, M., DeJong, W., O'Doherty, C., & Jernigan, D. (2015). Beverage- and Brand-Specific Binge Alcohol Consumption among Underage Youth in the U.S. *Journal of substance use*, *20*(5), 333–339.

Nation M, Crusto C, Wandersman A, Kumpfer KL, Seybolt D, Morrissey-Kane E, Davino K. What works in prevention: Principles of effective prevention programs. *Am Psychol.* 2003;58(6-7):449–456

National Collaborating Centre for Mental Health (UK). Alcohol-Use Disorders: Diagnosis, Assessment and Management of Harmful Drinking and Alcohol Dependence. *Leicester (UK): British Psychological Society; 2011.* (NICE Clinical Guidelines, No. 115.) 2, Alcohol dependence and harmful alcohol use

National Highway Traffic Safety Administration (NHTSA) 2001: Community How To Guide on Underage Drinking Enforcement, Guide 5

National Institute of Alcohol Abuse and Alcoholism(NIAAA) 2006: Underage Drinking Alcohol Alert, Nov 67.

National Institute on Alcohol Abuse and Alcoholism (NIAAA). (2003, April). Underage drinking: A major public health challenge. *Alcohol Alert, 59.*

National Institute on Drug Abuse (*NIDA*). (2003). Preventing drug abuse among children and adolescents: A research-based guide for parents, educators and community leaders (2nd ed.).

National Institutes of Health(webpage): National Institute on Drug Abuse (*NIDA*)

National Research Council (US) and Institute of Medicine (US) Committee on Integrating the Science of Early Childhood Development; Shonkoff JP, Phillips DA, editors. From Neurons to Neighborhoods: The Science of Early Childhood Development. *Washington (DC): National Academies Press (US)*; 2000. 13

National Research Council and Institute of Medicine (2009). Preventing mental, emotional, and behavioral disorders among young people: Progress and possibilities. *Washington, DC: National Academies Press*; 2009.Norusis M (2011): *IBM SPSS Statistics 19 Advanced Statistical Procedures Companion, Ch 4 Ordinal Regression*

Neighbors, C., Larimer, M. E., Lostutter, T. W., & Woods, B. A. (2006). Harm reduction and individually focused alcohol prevention. *The International journal on drug policy*, 17(4), 304–309. doi:10.1016/j.drugpo.2006.05.004

NIAAA (2006). Underage drinking: Why do adolescents drink, what are the risks, and how can underage drinking be prevented? *Alcohol Alert, 67.*

NIAAA (2009): Alcohol Alert, A Development Perspective on Underage Alcohol Use, Number 78, July 2009, *US Department of Health and Human Services*

NIAAA Newsletter. Vol. 3. Washington, DC: NIAAA; Winter. 2004

NIDA(2003): Preventing Drug Use Among Children and Adolescents, A Research Based guide for parents, Educators, and Community Leaders.

NIDA(2010): Comorbidity: Addiction and Other Mental Illnesses. *Research Report Series. US DHHS*

NIDA(2016): Principles of Substance Abuse Prevention for Early Childhood: A research-Based Guide Bränström et al 2008

Norusis M (2011): IBM SPSS Statistics 19 Advanced Statistical Procedures Companion, chap. 4 Ordinal Regression.

OECD (2015), Tackling Harmful Alcohol Use: Economics and Public Health Policy, OECD Publishing. http//dx.doi.org/10.1787/9789264181069-en

OECD (2020), Alcohol consumption (indicator). doi: 10.1787/e6895909-en (Accessed on 15 March 2020)

Office of National Drug Control Policy(ONDCP) and Substance Abuse and Mental Health Services(SAMSHA) (2012): Screening, Brief Intervention, and Referral to Treatment(SBIRT). Fact Sheet. *The White House*

Organization for Economic Co-operation and Development (OECD). (2013). *OECD Factbook 2013. Economic, Environmental and Social Statistics, OECD.*

PAHO(2015): Regional Status Report on Alcohol and Health in the Americas. Washington, DC : PAHO, 2015

Patel, V., Flisher, A., Hetrick, S., and McGorry, P. (2007, April 14). Mental health of young people: A global public-health challenge. *Lancet, 396* (9569), 1302–13.

Patrick ME, Schulenberg JE(2013). Prevalence and predictors of adolescent alcohol use and binge drinking in the United States. *Alcohol Res.* 2013;35(2):193–200. PubMed PMID: 24881328; PubMed Central PMCID: PMC3908711

Pedersen W and von Soest(2015): Adolescent Alcohol Use and Binge Drinking: An 18-Year Trend Study of Prevalence and Correlates, *Alcohol and Alcoholism*, Volume 50, Issue 2, March/April 2015, Pages 219–225

Petraitis, J., Flay, B.R. and Miller, T.Q. (1995) Reviewing theories of adolescent substance use: Organizing pieces in the puzzle. *Psychological Bulletin*, 117, 67–86. http://dx.doi.org/10.1037/0033–2909.117.1.67

Poikolainen K(2000). Risk factors for alcohol dependence: a case-control study. *Alcohol* 2000;35(2):190–196.

Popova S, Rehm J, Patra J, Zatonski W. Comparing alcohol consumption in central and eastern Europe to other European countries. *Alcohol* 2007;42(5):465–473. doi: 10.1093/alcalc/agl124

Rehm J., Zatonksi W., Taylor B., Anderson P(2011): Epidemiology and alcohol policy in Europe. *Addiction* 2011; 106: 11–19

Rehm, J. (2011). The risks associated with alcohol use and alcoholism. *Alcohol Research and Health, 34*(2), 135–143.

Rehm, J., & Imtiaz, S. (2016). A narrative review of alcohol consumption as a risk factor for global burden of disease. *Substance abuse treatment, prevention, and policy*, 11(1), 37. doi:10.1186/s13011-016-0081-2

Rehm, J., Allamani, A., Elekes, Z., Jakubczyk, A., Manthey, J., Probst, C.,. Wojnar, M. (2015). Alcohol dependence and treatment utilization in Europe: A representative cross-sectional study in primary care. *BMC Family Practice*, 16 (90), 1–9.

Rehm, J., Dawson, D., Frick, U., Gmel, G., Roerecke, M., Shield, K., and Grant, B. (2014). Burden of disease associated with alcohol use disorders in the United States. *Alcoholism: Clinical and Experimental Research*, 38(4), 1068–1077.

Rehm, J., Gmel, G. E., Sr, Gmel, G., Hasan, O., Imtiaz, S., Popova, S., Probst, C., Roerecke, M., Room, R., Samokhvalov, A. V., Shield, K. D., & Shuper, P. A. (2017). The relationship between different dimensions of alcohol use and the burden of disease-an update. *Addiction (Abingdon, England), 112*(6), 968–1001. https://doi.org/10.1111/add.13757

Rehm, J., Mathers, C., Popova, S., Thavorncharoesnap, M., Teerawattananon, Y., and Patra, J. (2009). Global burden of disease and injury and economic cost attributable to alcohol use and alcohol use disorders. *Lancet, 373*, 2223–33.

Rehm, J., Room, R., Graham, K., Monteiro, M., Gmcl, G., and Sempos, C. (2003). The relationship of average volume of alcohol consumption and patterns of drinking to burden of disease: An overview. *Addiction, 98*, 1209–1228.

Rehm, J., Room, R., Monteiro, M., Gmel, G., Graham, K., Rehn, N., . . . Jernigan, D. (2004). Alcohol Use. In M. Ezzati, A. Lopez, A. Rodgers, and C. Murray (Eds.), *Comparative quantification of health risks: Global and regional burden of disease due to selected major risk factors (Vol. 1, pp. 959–1108).* Geneva: World Health Organization (WHO).

Rehm, J., Shield, K., Rehm, M., Gmel, G., and Frick, U. (2012). *Alcohol consumption, alcohol dependence, and attributable burden of disease in Europe: Potential gains from effective interventions for alcohol dependence.* Centre for Addiction and Mental Health (CAMH). Toronto, ON

Resnick, M., Bearman, P., Blum, R., Bauman, K., Harris, K., Jones, J., . . . Udry, J. (1997). Protecting adolescents from harm: Findings from the National Longitudinal Study on Adolescent Health. *Journal of the American Medical Association, 278*(10), 823—832.

Rohde P, Lewinsohn PM, Kahler CW, Seeley JR, Brown RA(2001). Natural course of alcohol use disorders from adolescence to young adulthood. *J Am Acad Child Adolesc Psychiatry.* 2001;40:83–90.

Romer D. (2010). Adolescent risk taking, impulsivity, and brain development: implications for prevention. *Developmental psychobiology*, 52(3), 263–276. doi:10.1002/dev.20442

Sacks J.J., Gonzales K.R., Bouchery E.E., Tomedi L.E., Brewer R.D. 2010 national and state costs of excessive alcohol consumption. *Am. J. Prev. Med.* 2015;49:e73–e79.

SAMHSA(Substance Abuse and Mental Health Services Administration (US); Office of the Surgeon General (US). 2016: Facing Addiction in America: The Surgeon General's Report on Alcohol, Drugs, and Health [Internet]. *Washington (DC): US Department of Health and Human Services;* 2016 Nov. CHAPTER 3, PREVENTION PROGRAMS AND POLICIES.

SAMHSA(Substance Abuse and Mental Health Services Administration)2014: Results From the 2013 National Survey on Drug Use and Health: Summary of National Findings. NSDUH Series H-48, HHS Publication SMA 14-4863. *Rockville, MD: Substance Abuse and Mental Health Services Administration;* 2014.

SAMHSA. (2014). *Results from the 2013 National Survey on Drug Use and Health: Mental Health Findings.* Substance Abuse and Mental Health Services Administration. Rockville, MD: Substance Abuse and Mental Health Services Administration.

Saunders JB; Aasland OG ; Babor TF ; de la Fuente JR ; Grant M.(1993) Development of the Alcohol Use Disorders Screening Test (AUDIT). *WHO collaborative project on early detection of persons with harmful alcohol consumption. II. Addiction*;88:791–804

Savell, E., Fooks, G., & Gilmore, A. B. (2016). How does the alcohol industry attempt to influence marketing regulations

Schor, E. (1996). Adolescent alcohol use: Social determinants and the case for early family-centered prevention. Family-focused prevention of adolescent drinking. *Bulletin of the New York Academy of Medicine, 73*, 335–356.

Sherry H. Stewart, Patricia J. Conrod, Antti Latvala et al(2012) : Prevention of Alcohol Use and Misuse in Youth: A Comparison of North American and European Approaches, Ch 3, P147-208 in Philippe De Witte and Mack C. Mitchell Jr. (ed.) Under age Drinking: A Report on Drinking in the Second Decade of Life in Europe and North America

Shonkoff JP, Garner AS, Committee on Psychosocial Aspects of, Child Family, Health et al. The lifelong effects of early childhood adversity and toxic stress. *Pediatrics.* 2012;129(1):e232–46.

Shonkoff, J. (2009). Mobilizing Science to Revitalize Early Childhood Policy. *Issues in Science and Technology*, 26(1), 79-85.

Shonkoff, J.P. and Bales, S.N. (2011). Science Does Not Speak for Itself: Translating Child Development Research for the Public and Its Policymakers. *Child Development*, 82 (1), 17-32.

Siegel MB, Naimi TS, Cremeens JL, Nelson DE. Alcoholic beverage preferences and associated drinking patterns and risk behaviors among high school youth. *Am J Prev Med* 2011;40(4):419–26. 10.1016/j.amepre.2010.12.011

Siqueira L., Smith V. C. Binge Drinking. *PEDIATRICS*. 2015;136(3):e718–e726. doi: 10.1542/peds.2015-2337.

Sloboda, Z., and David, S. (1997). *Preventing drug use among children and adolescents: A research-based guide*. National Clearinghouse for Alcohol and Drug Information.

Slutske WS(2005). Alcohol Use Disorders Among US College Students and Their Non–College-Attending Peers. *Arch Gen Psychiatry*. 2005;62(3):321–327. doi:10.1001/archpsyc.62.3.321

Spoth R.L., Redmond C., Lepper H.(1999) Alcohol initiation outcomes of universal family-focused preventive interventions: one- and two-year follow-ups of a controlled study. *J. Stud. Alcohol*. 1999;13:103–111

Squeglia LM, Jacobus J, Tapert SF (2014). The effect of alcohol use on human adolescent brain structures and systems. *Handb Clin Neurol*. 2014; 125:501–10. doi: 10.1016/B978-0-444-62619-6.00028-8. PubMed PMID: 25307592; PubMed Central PMCID: PMC4321715.

Steinberg, L. (2008). A social neuroscience perspective on adolescent risk-taking. *Developmental Review*, 28, 78–106.

Steinberg, L. (2012). Should the science of adolescent brain development inform public policy? *Issues in Science and Technology, Spring*, 67–78.

Stewart S.H., Conrod P.J., Marlatt G.A., Comeau M.N., Thush C., and Krank M. (2005), "New developments in prevention and early intervention for alcohol abuse in youths." *Alcoholism: Clinical and Experimental Research*, 29(2), 278–286. "Is

Stigler, M., Neusel, E., and Perry, C. (2011). School-based programs to prevent and reduce alcohol use among youth. *Alcohol Research and Health, 34*, 157–62.

Stockings E, Hall WD, Lynskey M, Morley KI, Reavley N, Strang J, Patton G, Degenhardt L(2016). Prevention, early intervention, harm reduction, and treatment of substance use in young people. *Lancet Psychiatry*. 2016 Mar;3(3):280–96. doi: 10.1016/S2215-0366(16)00002-X

Storr CL, Pacek LR(2013), Martins SS. Substance use disorders and adolescent psychopathology. *Public Health Reviews*. 2013;34:1–42.

Strøm, H. K., Adolfsen, F., Fossum, S., Kaiser, S., & Martinussen, M. (2014). Effectiveness of school-based preventive interventions on adolescent alcohol use: a meta-analysis of randomized controlled trials. *Substance abuse treatment, prevention, and policy*, 9, 48. doi:10.1186/1747-597X-9-48

Stuckler, D, Basu, S, Suhrcke, M, Coutts, A, and McKee, M (2009): The public health effect of economic crises and alternative policy responses in Europe: an empirical analysis. *Lancet*.; 374: 315–323

Substance Abuse and Mental Health Services Administration (US)(2016); Office of the Surgeon General (US). Facing Addiction in America: The Surgeon General's Report on Alcohol, Drugs, and Health [Internet]. Washington (DC): US Department of Health and Human Services; 2016 Nov. CHAPTER 3, PREVENTION PROGRAMS AND POLICIES. Available from:

Sudhinaraset, M., Wigglesworth, C., & Takeuchi, D. T. (2016). Social and Cultural Contexts of Alcohol Use: Influences in a Social-Ecological Framework. *Alcohol research : current reviews*, 38(1), 35–45.

Swendsen, J., Conway, K. P., Degenhardt, L., Glantz, M., Jin, R., Merikangas, K. R., Sampson, N., … Kessler, R. C. (2010). Mental disorders as risk factors for substance use, abuse and dependence: results from the 10-year follow-up of the National Comorbidity Survey. *Addiction (Abingdon, England)*, 105(6), 1117–28.

The Science of Early Childhood Development(2007): National Scientific Council on the Developing Child. http://www.developingchild.net

Toumbourou, J., Stockwell, T., Neighbors, C., Marlatt, G., Sturge, J., and Rehm, J. (2007). Interventions to reduce harm associated with adolescent substance use. *Lancet, 369, 1391–401.*

U.S. Department of Health and Human Services (HHS)(2016), Office of the Surgeon General, Facing Addiction in America: *The Surgeon General's Report on Alcohol, Drugs, and Health. Washington, DC: HHS, November 2016.*

UNICEF Office of Research. (2013). *Child well-being in rich countries: A comparative overview. Florence, Italy: UNICEF Office of Research.*

United Nations (2019): The Sustainable Development Goals Report 2019

Viner RM, Taylor B. Adult outcomes of binge drinking in adolescence: findings from a UK national birth cohort. *J Epidemiol Community Health.* 2007 Oct;61(10):902-7. doi: 10.1136/jech.2005.038117. PMID: 17873228; PMCID: PMC2652971.

Wandersman A, Duffy J, Flaspohler P, Noonan R, Lubell K, Stillman L, et al(2008). Bridging the gap between prevention research and practice: the interactive systems framework for dissemination and implementation. *Am J Community Psychol.* 2008;41(3–4):171–181.

Wechsler, H., & Nelson, T. F. (2010). Will increasing alcohol availability by lowering the minimum legal drinking age decrease drinking and related consequences among youths?. *American journal of public health*, 100(6), 986–992.

Whiteford, H., Degenhardt, L., Rehm, J., Baxter, A., Ferarri, A., Erskine, H., . . . Vos, T. (2013, November 9). Global burden of disease attributable to mental and substance use disorders: Findings from the global burden of disease study 2010. *Lancet, 328* (9904), 1575–1586.

WHO (2014d): Disease Burden Estimates for 200–2012, *Geneva WHO*

WHO(2013): Status Report on Alcohol and Health in 35 European Countries 2013, *Regional office of Europe.*

WHO(2014a): The Global Status Report on Alcohol and Health, *Geneva WHO*

WHO(2018): Global Status Report on Alcohol and Health.

WHO(2019): Status report on alcohol consumption, harm and policy responses in 30 European countries 2019, September 2019, *Alcohol-consumption-harm-policy-responses-30-European-countries-2019.pdf*

WHO. (2004). Summary report: Prevention of mental disorders: Effective interventions and policy options. *Geneva: WHO.*

WHO. (2010a). Global status report on non-communicable diseases. *Geneva: WHO.*

WHO. (2010b). ATLAS on substance use: Resources for the prevention and treatment of substance use disorders. *Geneva: WHO.*

WHO. (2011). Global status report on alcohol and health.

WHO. (2014b). Social determinants of mental health. *Geneva WHO*

WHO. (2014c): The global status report on non-communicable diseases 2014, *Geneva WHO.*

Williams W (2016) Understanding and interpreting generalized ordered logit models, *The Journal of Mathematical Sociology*, 40:1, 7-20, DOI: 10.1080/0022250X.2015.1112384

Williams, R. A., & Quiroz, C. (2019). Ordinal Regression Models. In P. Atkinson, S. Delamont, A. Cernat, J.W. Sakshaug, & R.A. Williams (Eds.), *SAGE Research Methods Foundations.* doi: 10.4135/9781526421036885901

Wills TA, Vaccaro D, McNamara G (1992) The role of life events, family support, and competence in adolescent substance use: a test of vulnerability and protective factors. *Am J Community Psychol 20: 349–374*

Windle M, Spear LP, Fuligni AJ, Angold A, Brown JD, Pine D, Smith GT, Giedd J, Dahl RE. Transitions into underage and problem drinking: developmental processes and mechanisms between 10 and 15 years of age. *Pediatrics. 2008 Apr;121 Suppl 4(Suppl 4):S273-89*

Windle, M., and Zucker, R. (2010). Reducing underage and young adult drinking: How to address critical drinking problems during this developmental period. *Alcohol Research and Health, 33(1–2), 29–44.*

Winters, K., Botzet, A., and Fahnhorst, T. (2011). Advances in adolescent substance abuse treatment. *Current Psychiatry Reports, 13(5), 416–421.*

Wolfson, M., Wagenaar, A. C., & Hornseth, G. W. (1995). Law officers' views on enforcement of the minimum drinking age: a four-state study. *Public health reports (Washington, D.C. : 1974), 110(4), 428–438.*

Wooldridge J(2013): Introductory Econometrics, A Modern Approach, 5th edition, *South-Western, Cengage Learning*

World Health Organization (WHO) (2001). The world health report 2001 — Mental health: New understanding, new hope. *Geneva: WHO.*

World Health Organization, United Nations Children's Fund, World Bank Group(2018): Nurturing care for early childhood development: a framework for helping children survive and thrive to transform health and human potential. *Geneva: World Health Organization; 2018.*

World Health Organization. (2010c). Global strategy to reduce the harmful use of alcohol

Wu SS, Ma C-X, Carter RL, Ariet M, Feaver EA, Resnick MB, et al. Risk factors for infant maltreatment: a population-based study. *Child Abuse Negl 2004;28:1253–64.*

Yoon, S., & Lam, T. H. (2013). The illusion of righteousness: corporate social responsibility practices of the alcohol industry. *BMC public health,* 13, 630. doi:10.1186/1471-2458-13-630

Yuma-Guerrero PJ, Lawson KA, Velasquez MM, von Sternberg K, Maxson T, Garcia 2012): Screening, brief intervention, and referral for alcohol use in adolescents: a systematic review. *Pediatrics 2012; 130:115–122.*

Zucker, R. A., Donovan, J. E., Masten, A. S., Mattson, M. E., & Moss, H. B. (2008). Early developmental processes and the continuity of risk for underage drinking and problem drinking. *Pediatrics, 121 Suppl 4(Suppl 4),* S252–S272. doi:10.1542/peds.2007-2243B

Printed in the United States
By Bookmasters